Smaimtang3

JIC X
(Ban)

185 346 8819

Internet
for All

185 346 8819

Internet
for All

David Banes and
Richard Walter

Second Edition

David Fulton Publishers
London

David Fulton Publishers Ltd
The Chiswick Centre, 414 Chiswick High Road, London W4 5TF

www.fultonpublishers.co.uk

First published in Great Britain in 2000 by David Fulton Publishers
Second edition 2002

Note: The rights of David Banes and Richard Walter to be identified as the authors of this work has been asserted by them in accordance with the Copyright, Designs and Patents Act 1988.

Copyright © David Banes and Richard Walter 2002

British Library Cataloguing in Publication Data
A catalogue record for this book is available from the British Library.

ISBN 1–85346–881–9

Typeset by Elite Typesetting Techniques Ltd, Eastleigh, Hampshire, UK
Printed in Great Britain by Bell & Bain Ltd., Glasgow

Contents

Introduction to Second Edition

Since we published this book almost two years ago, the growth of the internet has continued apace. Society has continued to respond to both the potential and the dangers of the Internet as a means of communication and interaction. The purpose of a second edition is to update and refresh the first and to offer new material gleaned in response to new ideas and thoughts.

The Internet is a force that is here to stay, the sheer diversity of applications that utilise the Web is proof of that. Contrary to what some people may think, the demise of some of the dot.com's and the reduction in 'free' services is in no way an indicator that the Web will fail. Instead it is is a sign that applications and services launched across the Web need to have a firm financial footing – just like any other services, and will need to have a clear customer base whose needs are met through the applications.

The disability movement is beginning to make extensive use of the Web, portals for that community are growing both in number and complexity (4DP.com, youreable.com, etc.) But we are also seeing an increase in usage of the Web for information and advice. AbilityNet – the UK charity focusing on matching the needs of people with a disability to mainstream technology – reported that in one month in 2001, 5,000 factsheets were downloaded from their website, increasingly more people receive their information in this format than in any other.

However the changes to the internet economy, occurring naturally, and as a result of the slowdown in the US post-September 11, have suggested that we need to update some of our materials and suggest further ways in which the usage of the Internet can be integrated into schools and classrooms for children with special needs.

David Banes and Richard Walter
January 2002

Chapter 1

Introducing the Internet

This book started in 1995. The authors had been asked to give a paper at an Acorn World show following the publication of *IT for All* (Banes and Coles 1994). We spoke about school development to support the development of IT skills among pupils. Towards the end of our talk, we discussed the potential that the Internet might offer pupils with learning difficulties. This caused heated debate in the seminar room with a number of the audience expressing their views forthrightly.

Being obstinate we set out to make our point more clearly. Through the design of our website and through training and publications, we tracked the development of the Internet offering examples of its use by children with complex needs.

We believe that the work has been successful, winning awards from Microsoft, Becta and most recently ChildNet International, with press coverage in both the local, national and specialist press. No one now denies the importance of the Internet as a medium for communication which impacts on all of us in our daily lives. This does therefore appear to be the right time to take stock of the progress that has been made and to consider the issues that using the Internet with pupils with learning difficulties has raised.

Our starting point remains, that the Internet is here to stay. As commerce moves into the Web in a major way we need to ensure that the pupils with whom we work are interacting with the medium in a meaningful way. However, in beginning this book we need to clarify some of our terms.

Introduction

Throughout this book we are making some fundamental assumptions, based upon our experience. We will assume that most readers have some experience of using a PC, and that these machines are using a version of Windows equivalent to Windows 95 or above. We are not going to offer examples of other platforms, although we are aware of the use of Apple and Acorn machines, and other operating systems including Linux. Our experience has shown that

What is the Internet?

users of those systems are more than capable of making the comparisons, and for simplicity, the use of a standard terminology based on Windows PCs is of value.

Imagine your desktop computer: it stands alone on your desk, or in your bedroom or wherever. You can take a long lead and connect it to another computer in another room in your home. With the right software or 'protocols' these two computers can 'talk' to each other, they can share devices and files. In connecting these two computers together you have created your first network.

- **A network** is a group of computers connected together via hardware and software. The computers in a network can communicate with each other allowing them to share data, files and programs.

Networks have tended to be a little more complex than this. In most networks one computer operates as the master computer or 'server' and all the other computers in the network are linked to it. This is known as an 'intranet'. The wires can be through cable or the telephone network, but all of these machines connect to the central server and are capable of interacting one with the other.

- **An 'internet'** is a group of two or more networks interconnected physically; capable of communicating and sharing data between any machine in any of the networks; able to act together as a single network.

The Internet takes this idea a stage further. It links together many servers and through telecommunications (phone lines, ISDN, satellite etc.) any computer with the correct interpreters/protocols can speak to any other.

- **The Internet** is a group of many networks connected throughout the world. They are all interconnected physically; capable of communicating and sharing data between each computer in each network; able to act together as a single network.

These ways of connecting computers together are critical to the success of the Internet in the future. The most common system in the UK at the time of writing is to connect to the Internet through a standard phone line (referred to as PSTN). This can be quite slow, not least as the data is converted from a digital signal into an analogue signal to make the journey. A faster connection to the Internet is achieved through ISDN (integrated service digital network) which allows the signal to remain digital throughout and thus achieves greater speeds. At the end of June 2000 BT released its ADSL service in selected regions around the country which offered still faster connection speeds and constant connection for a flat fee.

Some schools are successfully using cable networks installed for cable TV and telephones, as a fast Internet connection. Some have begun to experiment with satellite connections. Satellite is likely to be a growth area in the future as it is not dependent on phone lines and physical connections.

Although the current major access to the Internet is through a desktop computer, this is likely to change as the telecommunications industry develops the principle of 'convergence' further. The term convergence refers to the anticipated fusing of a variety of media and telecommunications technologies into one seamless entity. Thus you could access e-mail through your telephone, your television programmes via your computer, web surf on your TV, etc. In practice this is likely to lead to single 'black boxes' that have sufficient capacity to perform all of these functions and others besides.

All of which is interesting background but leaves us with the question as to how all of this actually works in practice.

To communicate with each other, every computer on the Internet must follow the same rules for transmitting and reading the signal. These rules are called protocols, the most important of which is TCP/IP (Transmission Control Protocol/Internet Protocol). Through this protocol all the data that is transmitted and received across the Internet is broken into smaller packets and then reassembled by the receiver. Regardless of what platform or software you are using, it must communicate by TCP/IP.

What does TCP do?

- breaks up data into packets that the network can handle efficiently;
- verifies that all the packets arrive at their destination;
- reassembles the data envelopes, and addresses the data, like moving house from one part of the country to another.

What does IP do?

- envelopes (or packages) and addresses the data;
- enables the network to read the envelope and forward the data to its destination;
- defines how much data can fit in a single 'envelope' (a packet).

What can we do on the Internet?

A steady stream of Hollywood movies have introduced many of us to the ideas of the Internet. On the screen the Internet is instantaneous, colourful, dangerous. It can be used to control the environment and is accessible to everyone. In real life the Internet is a little more mundane.

The technology that creates the Internet is exciting, but the value of the Internet lies in how we might make use of this technology.

Using the protocols, we can use the Internet as a means by which we can communicate and interact. Ultimately the Internet provides new tools by which we can establish social, business and personal contact. The different tools that we have available to us include:

E-mail – allows information to be sent between computers.
FTP – allows files to be transferred between computers.
Chat/Messaging – text telephony session or messages.
Internet Videophone – allow text and video telephony over the Internet.
World Wide Web – system for providing, organising and accessing a wide variety of resources.

Let us look at each of these in turn.

E-mail (Electronic-mail)

E-mail is for many the first contact with the Internet. It allows us to write letters and 'post' them electronically to one or more named addresses. The address is usually made up of a personal name and the name of the Internet service provider. Hence a school e-mail address could be School@service.com.

E-mail can be accessed in two ways, either though a special dedicated software programme such as Eudora or Outlook Express, or through a special website that is accessed with your web browser.

Originally e-mail was text only; we wrote letters and sent them to each other. Conventions arose as the communication was often instant. Typing in capital letters was a form of 'shouting', emotions could be expressed by combinations of punctuation **:)** (happy) or **: (** (sad) etc. Sending abusive e-mail was referred to as flaming and unwanted e-mail was 'Spam'.

As the technology has advanced and use of the Internet has become more widely available some of these conventions have fallen by the wayside, but they still appear in some e-mails. Equally, e-mail has increasingly become multimedia. This extension has taken a number of forms. Most e-mail software can send attachments to your text. These can be pictures or sounds or even animations or video clips. However, increasingly the whole document can be sent as a multimedia production with animations, sounds and pictures embedded into the e-mail itself. Figures 1.1 and 1.2 show screens from different e-mail providers.

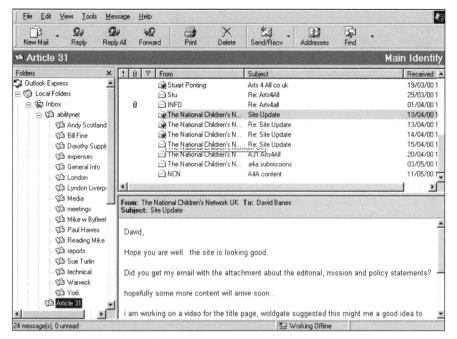

Figure 1.1 A screen shot from Outlook Express

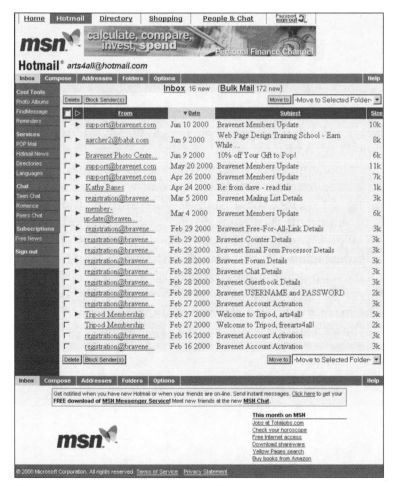

Figure 1.2 A screen shot from Hotmail

The technology that created e-mail also made available Newsgroups, by which a message or picture, etc. can be posted to an electronic bulletin board which people with similar interests can access.

Although the World Wide Web in many cases has supplanted Newsgroups, they still provide an excellent means of sending out messages which groups of people read and respond to.

View from the user

E-mail has been a valuable tool for allowing pupils with disabilities to communicate with the widest possible range of peers. Adults with disabilities have commented that the use of e-mail has opened up a wider range of employment possibilities as electronic text can be symbolised or spoken through the use of a screen-reader.

There can be little doubt that e-mail has rapidly become an important means of communication between people both in business and among friends. The growth of use is evident by the near panic caused by the release of new viruses (Melissa, 1999, or The Love Bug, early 2000), or perhaps by the increasing convergence of e-mail with mobile communications, most particularly the introduction of WAP (Wireless Application Protocol) phones in which both speech and text messages are increasingly available through a direct connection or across the Internet.

FTP – File Transfer Protocol

FTP is the set of rules that allows whole files to be sent or 'uploaded or downloaded' to another computer. FTP simply transfers the file from computer to computer; it does not read or display that file.

This can be very useful if you know exactly what file you want from a public FTP site, for instance Microsoft would allow downloads of important files from an FTP site as it is quite fast. Equally FTP allows you to store your own files onto a server or another computer, again a useful way of distributing files to others or keeping a back-up of important data.

FTP sites can be password protected to limit access, or some folders can be made public and others private, etc.

Figure 1.3 shows a simple layout of an FTP program.

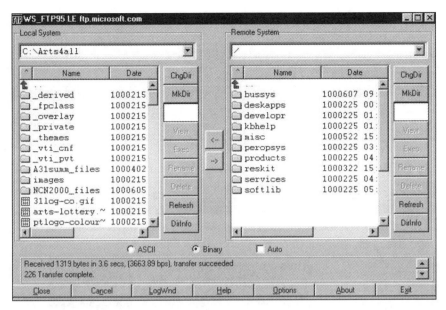

Figure 1.3 A screen shot of WS_FTP95

View from the user

FTP has been valuable to teachers, especially IT coordinators, as it allows them to update software, especially the operating system, very quickly. Whenever a computer is upgraded, there may be compatibility problems among the components. The ability to find the latest device drivers from an FTP site can save hours or even weeks of frustration.

Chat/messaging

Internet chat has been a growth area for many people, allowing them to 'talk' in real time live to others who share their interests around the world. The most widely used system is known as Inter Relay Chat (IRC) and this allows users to speak directly with a named person if both are online at the same time, or to join a chat room where a range of people are gathered together to talk about anything of mutual interest. Figure 1.4 shows a Yahoo chat screen.

Such chats have been enhanced by the ability to add pictures to the discussion or make small diagrams on a whiteboard, thus making communication between groups and individuals more transparent.

Internet chats have been still further augmented more recently by the introduction of avatars. These are cartoon characters, which can move through a virtual environment or text and interact by waving, smiling, etc.

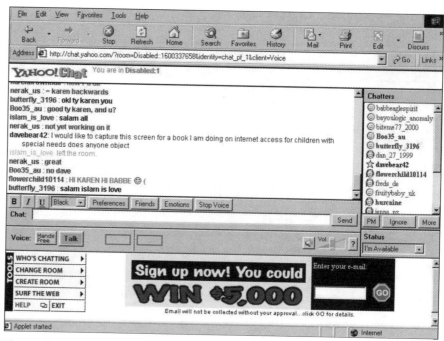

Figure 1.4 A chat screen

View from the user

Adults with disabilities have found online chat to be an immensely useful way of making and sustaining contact within a community. This has been especially valuable for those with speech difficulties as they can chat using text or graphics. Chat also has value for those with disabilities in that they can choose whether or not to disclose their disability depending on the community in which they wish to take part.

Variations upon a theme

There are various kinds of chat:

- HTML chat – embedded into the code of a webpage;
- Java chat – a small programme that runs within your webpage;
- IRC chat – a separate programme that operates independently of any other Internet application.

Text-based chat
Uses your own browser and lets you communicate live with other people over the Internet using text usually shown in different windows. The text can be spoken by an add on to the browser (see Figure 1.4).

Graphical chat
Allows you to use a graphical character (an avatar) to chat; it will probably use a Java-enabled browser.

Instant messaging

Uses a browser to chat over the Internet in real time. Java chat needs a Java-enabled browser – not recommended if you have an old browser or a slow modem. An example of a webchat browser can be found at: http://www.netguide.com/special/internet/chat/howto/types.html

Internet relay chat lines

Internet relay chat provides a way of communicating in real time with people from all over the world using a computer connected to the Internet. IRC is a multi-user, multi-channelled chatting system; you can talk through typed messages with one or more groups of people from all over the Internet in real time.

ICQ

ICQ (I seek you) is an Internet tool that informs you who's online at any time. With ICQ you can chat, send messages, files or URLs and play games with people all over the Internet. You can get a copy of ICQ from http://www.icq.com/products/whatisicq.html.

ICQ is a text-based program which allows you to send messages and to chat with other people. It also enables you to invite other people to chat with you using voice or video.

The following list of ICQ programs and recommendations is taken from the Northamptonshire People First website (http://www.peoplefirst.org.uk/). Northamptonshire People First is an organisation run by people with learning difficulties set up to help people with learning difficulties speak up for themselves.

- Qtalk: This is a program which has been designed so that ICQ users can use speech. Using it you can talk to people from around the world over the Internet. It is only available for PC users using Windows 95 or 98.
- HoneyQ: This is another Windows 95 or 98 program which allows voice and video conferencing over the Internet for people who use ICQ.
- Netmeeting: This is a PC program, which allows you to chat using text, voice and video.
- RocketTalk: This is a useful program as it allows you to send voice messages rather than having to type up an e-mail message. Moreover, it is free. This is an important program as it helps make the Internet accessible to many more people. Voice messages are great to listen to as well.

We recommend that you start by downloading the ICQ, QTalk, HoneyQ, Netmeeting and RocketTalk programs. You will then be ready to take part in an online conference.

Figures 1.5a and b show two setup screens for ICQ users.

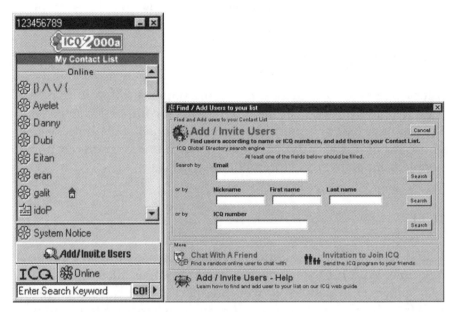

Figure 1.5a   Easy setup for ICQ

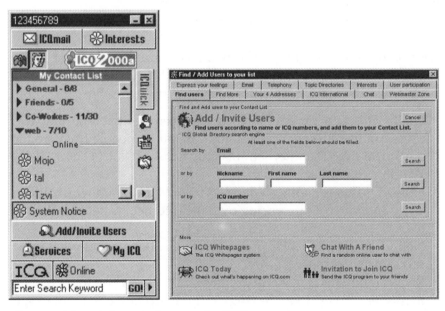

Figure 1.5b   Advanced setup for ICQ

All the access devices mentioned above can be used to support the computer chat rooms: overlay boards using set vocabulary and on-screen selection set grids (using Clicker, Windows switch).

As use of the Internet has grown and the technology has advanced, increasingly users have wanted to enhance the social experience of being connected. One of the major ways in which this has happened is by sending live stills or video clips of oneself while speaking or writing online. The cost of the camera has dropped dramatically over the past three years, but their use demands a very fast Internet connection at both ends of the communication (ISDN at least).

Videophones/ webcams

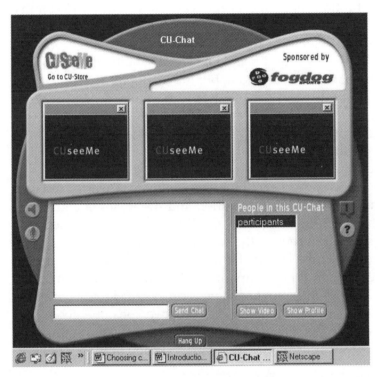

Figure 1.6   A blank CuSeeMe screen waiting for a webcam to go live

View from the user

Most users of the Web report that the video is too slow to be of great value. But research using ISDN and more recently cable and ADSL lines is being carried out to explore the use of remote support to people with a disability for refining switch use or updating computer setups.

Ultimately, the best-known application on the Internet is the World Wide Web (or WWW, W3 or just the Web for short). The Web is the fulfilment of the multimedia capability of the Internet.

The Web is made up of millions of individual sites, each of which is made up of one or more pages of information. This information can be viewed through a piece of software known as a browser. A browser reads a page written in HTML (hypertext markup language)

World Wide Web

and draws together any linked files and displays that page on your computer. The linked files may be text, pictures, sounds, animations graphics, video, etc.

Anyone can create a website and we will discuss this later in the book. The Web is therefore the equivalent of a huge electronic library, in which anyone can write whatever they like and publish it for others to see. As such it is open to abuse, both obscene and libellous. However, definitions of both concepts vary from country to country and culture to culture, and the Web is intrinsically worldwide.

This anarchic element to the Web provides both an opportunity and a threat for schools and people with a disability. Information is available to us if we wish to find it, but it may not be in a format that is accessible to us. Design of sites can make access easy or impossible.

Information can be about any topic one chooses to imagine from fly-fishing on the Danube to the Spice Girls, from aeroplanes to parasitic worms. Finding what we want can be difficult.

Facilities on the Web are rapidly becoming more powerful and uses for the technology besides information and discussion are growing. Medical advice can be sought on the Internet. When a colleague's computer crashed recently, the drivers needed for repair were downloaded from an FTP site. However the greatest area is that of e-commerce. We can do our supermarket shopping on the Internet, buy Christmas presents, purchase a pension, book a holiday, etc. This technology is changing the ways in which we consume goods and services on a daily basis. Figures 1.7 and 1.8 illustrate two of the news and commerce sites currently being used by many of those online.

Figure 1.7   Freeserve portal, 10 June 2000

Figure 1.8   The Times Online, 10 June 2000. © Times Newspapers Limited 2000

View from the user

The Web has been a valuable tool for people with disabilities. The sharing of information and support (see Figure 1.9), the extension of online support groups, along with the ability to access the knowledge base of research groups and the ability to buy online, have all enhanced the experience of those using the Internet. These issues will be discussed in much greater detail later in the book.

Convergence

All of the applications discussed above are converging into the multimedia attributes of the Web. Individual websites can have e-mail capabilities, public or private chat rooms, they may have viewable webcams, or bulletin boards, guestbooks and forums through which visitors can interact with the creators of the site and with each other. Files may be downloaded or uploaded by FTP through the site, etc.

The advent of broadband

One of the phrases that is referred to regularly in Internet circles is 'Broadband'. Broadband is in many ways the holy grail of Internet usage – fast, permanent and reliable connections to the Internet. Broadband is, if you like, a wider pipe through which data can be sent directly to your computer, the analogy is less effective in that this pipe is two-way, with data flowing in both directions. It is common for UK broadband providers to offer speeds of up to 10× a standard modem through ADSL and cable.

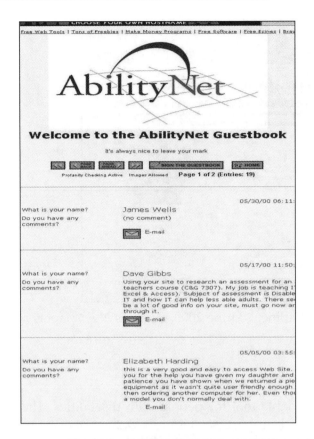

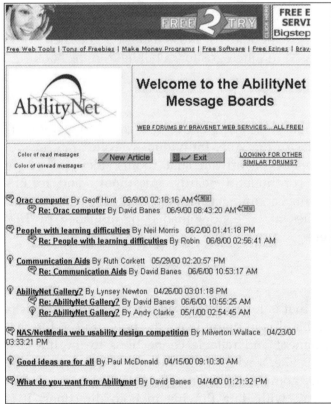

Figure 1.9 Web based guestbook and discussion forum – http://www.abilitynet.co.uk

ADSL

ADSL utilises existing phone lines to deliver fast services; specialist installation is required and it runs in parallel to your standard phone services. The most widely used ADSL provider is BT openworld.

Cable

Cable uses the networks set up to support cable TV to deliver equally fast data communications; in this case a separate connection point will need to be installed with a suitable cable modem. The most common cable provider in the UK is NTL.

View from the user

Broadband brings with it speed of data, allowing video, audio, graphics and text to be relayed at high speed. Such connections mean that remote support to individuals becomes a real possibility and the potential for low cost global audio or video conferencing a realistic option.

For example a young woman from Canada contacted one of the authors and mentiond the pain she experienced whilst typing. A webcam was set up in Canada and using video conferencing software her workstation was reviewed and changes made to her keyboard monitor and pointing device which considerably reduced her discomfort.

Similarly 'Paltalk', an application which brings together streaming text, video and audio onto the desktop, allows users to chat and see each other in real time online. At the time of writing two groups were available on line, one dealing with mental health issues and a second on multiple sclerosis.

Conclusion

As we discuss the use of the Internet by and for young people with disabilities we are aware that the Web is here to stay. Every TV advert or film trailer carries a linked site. You can listen to the radio across the Internet and read international daily newspapers. The challenge for schools is to make the Web meaningful for the children we work with, to make it safe and to utilise the capacity that the Web embraces to offer enhanced and exciting teaching and learning in the classroom.

The advent of broadband brings the convergence of these elements through a fixed connection closer together. As I type, my computer is downloading software for me to use to make screenshots. If this book were available in electronic form, live links could be established which would allow me to follow up on an area of interest through the Web simply by clicking on the relevant link. The speed of connection would open those pages up rapidly and thus enhance the text in a meaningful manner.

At the end of the day the use of the Internet is about the skill of the teacher; it cannot replace the teacher, it is merely a resource for us to use.

Chapter 2

Using the Internet with children: safe surfing

The Internet is a fascinating place. Compared to many media it is relatively uncensored, and by virtue of its democratic nature we can post just about anything we want onto a webpage.

In entering into this debate we are wary of opening the issue of censorship without any intention of offering definitive guidance. We would first comment that even within Europe there are huge variations as to what is considered inappropriate material. When we delivered lectures to staff in Denmark it was made quite clear to us that the pornography debate was of no real concern to them. However, we are well aware that any technology which limits access to websites can be used to protect, or conversely it can be used to limit freedom. A piece of software that says you may not visit www.sex.com can also be used to say that you may not visit www.freespeech.com or www.christian.com.

For some this causes concern. As one surfs one may come across material that is not appropriate to be viewed in schools. Or as a parent, you may spot material you would not wish your children to see. There is no certain way to protect children on an individual basis but there is a range of systems that schools or parents may use to increase the degree of control they exert over a child's viewing habits. One of the best sites if you wish to know more about these issues is http://www.safekids.com.

Browsers for children

One interesting aspect of developing tools for children to use is the creation of child-friendly browsers with simplified controls and built-in forms of filtering (e.g. Surf Monkey, Figure 2.1). The filtering can include objectionable phrases in chat rooms as well as images, etc.

Figure 2.1   Surf Monkey

Filtering

Blacklists

Possibly the best-known systems for limiting the use of the Net are blacklist programs. These store a list of inappropriate sites on a central server, which filters any URL that a child tries to visit. They are effective in blocking access to these sites, but in practice parents/teachers rely upon the list of sites being maintained and also on the standards applied by the censor being the same as those of the family or school. In practice, webmasters can think of names for sites faster than censors can find them.

Whitelists

Whitelists are more effective in limiting surfing in that they create a list of sites that are the only ones which can be visited by a child. While they successfully limit access to inappropriate material they also limit hugely the breadth of material that one can visit and it may be very frustrating if the same machine is used by both child and adult.

Other systems

Software can be purchased which limits the accessibility of sites according to different criteria. One such program works by detecting the amount of flesh tone on a given image and deciding if this is inappropriate. This criterion allowed visits to a site featuring couples having sex in PVC and leather but would not allow access to pages about swimming. The somewhat ludicrous nature of this software is self-evident.

A summary of the range of tools available for protecting children is available at http://www.microweb.com/pepsite/Software/filters.html.

One of the key issues with much of the software discussed above is the degree of policing of the child that is taking place. For parents, software can be used to send logs of all activity to a parental computer, but for many parents this is an uncomfortable decision to take. However, such log-keeping software may be more appropriate in a school setting where the issues of trust and accountability may be somewhat different. In one case a school was notified of a staff member's inappropriate use of the Web by a colleague of the person concerned. The logfile kept within the browser's history folder, coupled with the automatic caching of images, meant that it was straightforward to corroborate this, leading to the resignation of the member of staff. It is worth noting in this case, that the school used RM Internet for Learning as its ISP. RM offers a filtered service, but this was not sufficient to deter in this example.

Sensible surfing

Ultimately, protecting children from what any society deems inappropriate is both simpler and more complex than just using software or an ISP claiming to protect on your behalf. As with any form of protection it is ultimately about communicating belief systems and encouraging openness about what they may stumble across in using the Net. Much of this can only be communicated through lengthy discussion and is best not treated as an ICT issue but as a wider discussion within PSHE. Similarly at home, this is just one of many things parents must talk to children about.

The issues around safety on the Web are myriad. A useful site is www.getnetwise.com which offers practical advice on a range of options to match individual needs. The site makes the point that there are no simple solutions and that for some there may be a preference for software tools, whilst for others an honour system or contract may be most effective.

The site offers thoughts on a number of issues and solutions including time limiting; filtering and blocking access to some sites, words, and/or images; access to sexually explicit material, graphic descriptions or images, or hate groups advocating bigotry or hatred; also graphic violence – violent images, language, bomb-building, etc., and criminal activity – promoting illegal activity.

Other categories which may require thought have included alcohol, games, advertising, politics, sports, etc. There are also issues around the use of personal information and the need to limit Outgoing Content by preventing kids from revealing personal information online. Browsers for Kids do not display inappropriate words or images. Kid-Oriented search engines perform limited searches or screen search results. Monitoring tools alert adults to online activity without blocking access.

Guidelines on talking about the Web

As with any other form of communication, we need to instil into children an awareness of how to protect themselves. One key point for them to learn is the need to keep personal information private. Our phone number, passwords, address, etc. can be shared with those we know, but one should be wary about sharing them with others. Requests for personal information by e-mail, etc. should not be replied to unless we know who is at the other end.

A reasonable question for older children to think about is why people want this information. Is it:

- to try to sell you things?
- to try to send you unwanted e-mail (Spam)?
- to sell or trade your information with another company?

Children and young adults may find that if they don't give out details they can't get access to a page or to a download, but they need to be aware of the risks. Most websites will have a privacy policy if you are asked to give information and this should be checked by parents and children together.

Key points for children

- Never give out your full name, address, phone number to anyone you don't know.
- Never give out your Internet password to anyone, even if they say they're from your Internet service.
- Never get together with anyone you 'meet' online without first checking with your parents. If they agree to the meeting, be sure it's in a public place and that your parents are present.

Guidelines for teachers

Some careful thought can greatly minimise any risk to the child and to the school. Class rules can help. An example of some class rules based upon the safekids.com site is:

- Never give out identifying information.
- Get to know the sites the class uses.
- Never allow a child to arrange a face-to-face meeting with another computer user without being accompanied.
- Never respond to messages or bulletin board items that are suggestive, obscene, belligerent, threatening, or make you feel uncomfortable. Encourage your children to tell you if they encounter such messages.
- Should you become aware of the transmission, use, or viewing of child pornography while online, immediately report this to the police.

- Remember that people online may not be who they seem. Because you can't see or even hear the person it is easy for someone to misrepresent themselves. Thus, someone indicating that 'she' is a '12-year-old girl' could in reality be a 40-year-old man.
- Be sure to make this a group activity. Keep the computer in a group room.

There are no certain ways to protect children entirely. But sensible and open use of the Internet will help hugely.

www.safekids.com advocates the establishment of contracts between child and parent; this can be easily adapted for use in schools, and outline some of the adult's obligations as well as the child's.

Contracts

Family Contract for Online Safety
Kid's Pledge

1. I will not give out personal information such as my address, telephone number, parents' work address/telephone number, or the name and location of my school without my parents' permission.
2. I will tell my parents right away if I come across any information that makes me feel uncomfortable.
3. I will never agree to get together with someone I 'meet' online without first checking with my parents. If my parents agree to the meeting, I will be sure that it is in a public place and bring my mother or father along.
4. I will never send a person my picture or anything else without first checking with my parents.
5. I will not respond to any messages that are mean or in any way make me feel uncomfortable. It is not my fault if I get a message like that. If I do I will tell my parents right away so that they can contact the service provider.
6. I will talk with my parents so that we can set up rules for going online. We will decide upon the time of day that I can be online, the length of time I can be online, and appropriate areas for me to visit. I will not access other areas or break these rules without their permission.
7. I will not give out my Internet password to anyone (even my best friends) other than my parents.
8. I will be a good online citizen and not do anything that hurts other people or is against the law.

I agree to the above

_____
Child sign here

I will help my child follow this agreement and will allow reasonable use of the Internet as long as these rules and other family rules are followed.

_____
Parent(s) sign here

Family Contract for Online Safety
Parents' Pledge

1. I will get to know the services and websites my child uses. If I don't know how to use them, I'll get my child to show me how.
2. I will set reasonable rules and guidelines for computer use by my children and will discuss these rules and post them near the computer as a reminder. I'll remember to monitor their compliance with these rules, especially when it comes to the amount of time they spend on the computer.
3. I will not overreact if my child tells me about a problem he or she is having on the Internet. Instead, we'll work together to try to solve the problem and prevent it from happening again.
4. I promise not to use a PC or the Internet as an electronic babysitter.
5. I will help make the Internet a family activity and ask my child to help plan family events using the Internet.
6. I will try get to know my child's 'online friends' just as I try get to know his or her other friends.

I agree to the above

_____
Parent(s)

I understand that my parent(s) has agreed to these rules and agree to help my parent(s) explore the Internet with me.

_____
Child sign here

Such contracts can be displayed alongside computers in school, adapted into symbol systems and included in the reviews of progress completed with each child.

Developing school use of the Internet – policy issues

The other protection issue that arises in using the Internet is inappropriate use of the service by staff. In discussing this with colleagues it is useful to compare standards with those related to other media. What are the school rules for personal phone calls?

What are the rules about using letterheads for non-school business? How would the school respond to a member of staff found to have pornographic magazines in a locker? The rules we apply to staff use of the Internet should be in keeping with the standards and ethos we have established in school for other forms of potential misuse.

Policy then need not be long or complex and may be incorporated into a staff handbook. At one school the rules for use are simple: 'If a member of staff is found to be using the Internet to visit sites that would bring the school into disrepute this would be a disciplinary matter.' Such clarity is essential if a school is to demonstrate clearly its expectations and standards.

In recent months guidance on school policies has been issued from various sources. Some of the most useful has been put on the Web by Kent LEA and Becta: (www.kented.org.uk/ngfl/policy.html) and (www.becta.org.uk/technology/infosheets/html/accuse.html)

Both sets of guidance build upon that issued by the Government, which covers areas such as as e-mail, chat and websites and has changed recently. Schools should obtain the DfES Superhighway Safety pack (green cover) and must note the additional guidance on the website: http://safety.ngfl.gov.uk.

All of the sets of guidance are of value and include much that is worthwhile to dicuss in schools. Becta offer the following as starting points:

The following points will encourage discussion and thinking around the range of issues that should be considered before writing your Acceptable Use Policy (AUP). These issues should be considered in the context of teaching and learning and any other systems and/or policies that operate in the school.

- Why does your school need an AUP?
- What are the educational benefits of using the Internet in an educational context, and how will learning be enhanced?
- How will the school ensure that pupils are protected from unsuitable material and that they use the equipment safely?
- How will pupils be educated to access and evaluate Internet content?
- How will e-mail be managed?
- Will the school have a website? If so, who will take responsibility for coordinating and publishing content?
- Will the school give access to chat rooms and newsgroups?
- Who will manage ICT system security and how will it be maintained?
- Will Internet access be given out-of-school hours to pupils and the community?
- How will the school deal with complaints?
- How often will the policy be reviewed and by whom?

In addition Becta go on to advise:
An AUP (Acceptable Use Policy) should include:

- a requirement that all potential users of the Internet understand basic conventions and navigation techniques before going online and accessing pages
- information reminding students that logs are kept of sites visited and why
- an undertaking by pupils to respect copyright and not to plagiarise others' work
- an agreement by users to download pages to personal floppy disks rather than to the machine's hard disk, and an explanation of why such restrictions are necessary
- permission for members of staff to check personal disks for viruses and unsuitable material
- a commitment that pupils will keep their personal details private and not make them available to others using the Internet
- a pledge by users not to attempt to access unsuitable material
- a reminder that the possession of certain types of unsuitable material can lead to prosecution by the police
- information on sanctions for violations of the agreed AUP and how this links to other school policies: for example, how bullying electronically imposes the same sanctions as face to face – this would be linked to the school's anti-bullying policy.

One of the challenges that then faces schools is to utilise the Internet to empower and liberate pupils, whilst acknowledging the risks and threats which are inevitably entwined. Schools walk a tightrope between unacceptable limitation and unrestricted freedom. At the heart of good practice is the need to codify common sense and good practice.

Looking back over the policies the authors have been responsible for in schools and beyond, the time taken and wasted in drawing up policy is painful to review. The Web is such a fast-moving medium that to attempt to overly legislate against all eventualities may create inertia in Internet use that limits the opportunities for children to too great an extent; we would strongly advise that if the policy is greater than two sides of A4 it is far too long.

Summary

Protecting children is a major issue for schools in the light of media spotlight and child protection issues. While it is for each school to make its own decisions regarding policy, we would strongly recommend that a policy is developed and is included within any parent partnership agreement that you are developing or reviewing.

Chapter 3

Using the World Wide Web for teaching and learning in school

When working with children with special needs we can use the Internet as a tool to support learning across the curriculum. But as the Internet increasingly impacts upon the daily life of children both in and out of school, there will be a need to begin to think about helping young people to understand some of the technology that they are encountering and using.

In developing this sequence of lessons, we felt that it was important not to lose track of the key principles that inform the development of all schemes of work within a school. In particular the following aspects provided the framework to guide our thinking.

The teaching of the Internet should:

- Be incorporated into the total communication policy at the school. (This includes the use of speech, signing, rebus symbols, written words, VOCA (Voice Output Communication Aids).)
- Be rooted in the concrete experience of pupils.
- Enable our pupils access to other individuals and groups through e-mail and special interest groups.
- Promote individual educational aims in the following cross-curricular areas:

Communication	English
Personal Social and Health Education	IT skills

- Promote access to English (Speaking and listening, Writing, Reading) within the curriculum.
- Be used to support the application of the National Curriculum with our pupils in various curriculum areas.
- Promote communication with individuals and groups outside school.
- Developing writing and communication skills. Involving following a process of: plan – draft – revise – proofread – present, and by making judgements about tone, style, format and choice of vocabulary as appropriate to the intended audience.

This chapter includes a number of lesson plans and practical classroom sessions that have been used to introduce the Internet to pupils at school on the basis of these principles.

Key features

We base all our teaching on ideas and concepts that are familiar to our pupils. At the start of every session we review some basic concepts about the Internet.

1. What is the Internet?
   The Internet is a large number of computers all over the world all linked together. They can pass information to each other. The information can be words, pictures or sounds.
2. What kind of different information is sent over the Internet?
   Information is sent as text, pictures, sounds and video.
3. How is information sent over the Internet?
   Information is sent between the computers on the Internet in small packages.
4. How is information sent to the right destination?
   Each package of information is addressed to the right person.

From this starting point the following progression of lesson (schemes of work) was developed.

Introducing the Internet

It can be interesting to look at some of the principles behind the Internet to help pupils understand how the Internet works.

Key concepts
What is the Internet?
How is the information sent and received over the Internet?
How does the information get to the right place on the Internet?
What sort of information can be sent over the Internet?

Resources
Magazine pictures and text.
Scissors, sugar paper, staples or Sellotape.
Optional: computer, Internet connection, telephone.

Outline
Making a model of the Internet
Construct a number of paper tubes from the sugar paper sheets.
Use these paper tubes to simulate the Internet superhighway down which information can pass.

Constructing the internet highway

The pupils then chose information to send, perhaps starting with A4 pictures of themselves printed from their digitised images. They chose who to send the data to on the other side of the Internet superhighway (the rolled up paper tubes).

Choosing data to send over our model internet

The full-sized pictures wouldn't fit down the 'internet tubes', so to pass this information down our internet superhighway/paper tubes the pictures were cut up into smaller data packages with 'electric scissors'.

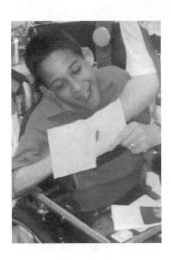 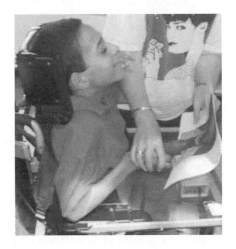

Preparing the data packages by cutting up the pictures

Once the pupils had cut the pictures up, they then had to get onto our model internet system. To make our model more representative of a real internet system we recorded distinctive telephone connection sounds. Each time pupils wanted to get onto the internet, they would use a switch to access a speech machine (or a tape recorder) which then produced the telephone connection sounds. They were then allowed to send their messages by posting them down the internet tube. The data in the form of the cut up pictures was received by the person on the other end of our internet link.

Sending the data   Receiving the data

The data received had then to be sorted and reconstructed from the constituent pieces to form the whole picture or text message.

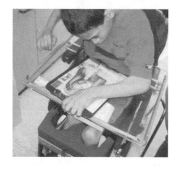 

Reconstructing the data into its original format

In subsequent sessions the pupils chose different types of information to send as data via their internet. Some chose drawings or written messages; some chose to write messages in symbolic form using 'Writing with Symbols'; some chose pictures from magazines.

They cut up their chosen message into pieces and sent it down our internet superhighway to their partners, who reconstructed the data into its original form.

This was successful when pupils sent information directly to one another but to make our model more realistic we then introduced the concept of a central server who receives all the data rom different individuals.

This central server had to sort all the incoming 'mail' to its destination and then redirect it to the correct person.

This was found to be possible if our model network wasn't too busy, but as the volume of traffic on our internet increased, the central server got inundated with bits of pictures and eventually couldn't keep up with the amount of information and who to send the various messages on to. Our model of the internet then became jammed.

This difficulty (internet jamming) was solved by introducing the concept of putting the data into packages (envelopes). Each of the data packages was addressed to the person to whom the information was sent.

The pupils first used a method of addressing the packages of data by writing the name of the person (or a code number) to whom they were sending data. They found this allowed the central server to sort and to send the data to the correct address even though our internet was very busy.

Additional concepts of error checking and data redundancy were introduced and discussed by thinking about what would happen if all the data was not all sent or received correctly.

Key concepts
HTML Markup programming:
The concepts behind using 'markups' to alter following events.

Resources
Action cards, markup cards. Programming sheets.
Paint, crayons, paintbrushes, paper.

Outline

The concept behind a markup language is that the markup is a way of altering what happens next.
For example 'Speaking'. You can speak loudly, softly, high or low.

Activity: markup:

| speak | | loudly | | softly | | high | | low |

So to speak softly you would combine:

| softly | | speak |

To speak low and softly you would combine:

| low | | softly | | speak |

You can build up programming cards to describe many activities.
For example   Drumming: hard/soft/quick/slow
              Painting: red/yellow/thick/thin

You can combine lots of markup instructions to influence one action for example:

   HTML 'markup' program   result in our 'web browser'

Red thick wavy *draw*   =

Pupils can make up their own hypertext markup programs and pass them to others who (acting as web browsers) can execute the instructions.
   One group acting as HTML programmers and the others as internet browsers interpreting the data.

Action	Markup 1	Markup 2	Markup 3
Shout	*loud*	*high*	*short*
Move	*quick*	*small*	*gentle*
Drum	*soft*	*fast*	*4/4 rhythm*

This can also illustrate an important feature of the HTML web language and the nature of Internet browsers.
The interpretation of the commands can vary between web browsers according to their internal settings. We can have different ideas of what constitutes a thick wavy line, or a loud noise.

Key concepts
HTML Markup programming:
The concept behind using 'markups' to alter following events.
Creating markup programs using dice.

Resources
Action dice, markup dice. Programming sheets.
Paint, crayons, paintbrushes, paper.

Outline

The concept behind a markup language is that the markup is a way of altering what happens next.
Make two sets of dice (or spinners).
One dice represents the activity.
One dice represents the markup.

Activity dice

Throw the activity dice to choose the activity:
In the example 'wave'

Then throw the markup dice to see how the activity is going to be effected.

Markup effect:

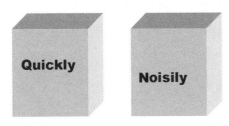

Complete markup program is
<QUICKLY> <NOISILY> <WAVE>

Pupils can construct their own markup programs, by throwing the markup dice and carrying out the instructions.

Further work on the concepts behind HTML

31

Exploring human and Internet communication

Key concepts
Investigating and comparing human and computer based forms of communication.
The Internet is another form of communication.

Resources
White board and pens.
Examples of different communication methods (telephones, morse code, etc.).

Outline
Investigate different methods of communication:

Ask pupils for all the different ways they know of communicating.
The list might include:
talking, shouting, writing, telephones, symbols, signing, semaphore, morse code and computers.

Practical investigations:
Which methods are best in different conditions?
For example:
Which methods are most successful in a noisy room?
gesticulating/signing, pictures/symbols, speaking/speech aids?
Which methods are most successful in a dark room?
gesticulating/signing, pictures/symbols, speaking/speech aids?
Which methods are best over long and over short distances?
Which methods are the most environmentally friendly?
How much does each method cost?
Which methods are the most cost effective?

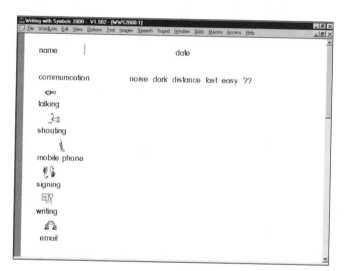

Sample from a possible recording form

Communication method	Noise	Dark	Distance	Fast	Easy	Other comments
Talking						
Shouting						
Mobile phone						
Signing						
Writing						
Email						

Key concepts
Using a web browser to surf the World Wide Web.

Resources
Computer with Internet connection. Web browser. Access devices as necessary. Information sheets.

Outline
Set pupils tasks or information to find out from the World Wide Web. An example of a search grid to search and to find out specific information.

Information to find	Websites I visited	How I found the websites	Number of websites	Time I took to find it
The recipe for 'carrot cake'	Recipes for Kids, Mayo clinic virtual cookbook	I searched for 'carrot cake' in Yahoo	There were 22 listed in Yahoo	5 minutes
Where is Robbie Williams playing next?	Robbie Williams' official site Robbie World	Searched in Altavista for 'Robbie Williams'	There were 33,121 pages in Altavista	4 minutes
Where do meercats live?				

Investigating
e-mail

Electronic mail (e-mail) is probably the most widely used part of the Internet. It allows you to send messages to anyone with an Internet connection faster, cheaper and more efficiently than ordinary postal mail. The messages do not have to consist purely of text, you can send graphics, pictures, sounds, music, data and even movie clips.

Key concepts
Investigating e-mail.
Comparisons with letter writing and telephoning (comparing the operation and formats of each method).
What are the advantages and disadvantages of e-mail over sending postal letters and telephoning?

Resources
White board, pen.
Computer, Internet connection, e-mail program.
Word or symbol processor.

Outline
Writing and receiving e-mails.

Comparisons with letter writing:
Writing a normal postal letter and an e-mail to the same address.
Sending both at the same time and comparing the time taken for them each to reach their destination and for a reply to be received.

Comparisons with telephoning:
Using e-mail and a telephone to contact someone.
Looking up telephone numbers, finding e-mail addresses.
Comparing ease of use, practicality of both methods.

	E-mail	Letter writing	Telephoning
Needs	Computer Internet link	Paper, pen, envelope stamp, postbox	Telephone Telephone link
Ease of use	Need to be able to operate a computer	You need to be able to write	You need to be able to speak
Time taken	Quick	Slow	Very Quick
Additional comments	Can use additional computer access devices. Need to be able to operate a computer	Need to be able to read and write. Need to buy a stamp and find a postbox	Need to be able to hear and talk. Need to be there and be awake. (time zones)

Table comparing e-mail, letter writing and telephoning

	requires	speed	ease	comments
e-mail				
letter				
telephone				

'Rebus' worksheet comparing e-mail, letter writing and telephoning

Further lessons on e-mail could include attaching pictures or sounds to e-mails or setting up e-mail contacts to schools either in this country or worldwide.

Using symbols in e-mail

There is a fully symbolic accessible e-mail program from Widgit computing called Inter_comm which is an addon to Writing with symbols 2000. Inter_comm has a completely text free interface to all e-mail functions:

• Photographic address book automatically updated.
• Symbol and text e-mails, using the writer's own style and choice of pictures.
• Send e-mails with your own pictures, which reappear just where you put them in the message.
• Automatic translation between Rebus and PCS symbols into the users preferred set.

You can learn more about Inter_comm from the Widgit website (www.widgit.com/).

Using symbols in e-mails is also possible using any e-mail program (Outlook Express, Eudora, etc.) when used in conjunction with Writing with Symbols 2000. Create your symbol writing in Writing with Symbols. You can use any additional access devices (overlay boards, switches, keyboard), alter the symbols as suits your pupils, add photos and speak out the text. Once the pupils are happy with

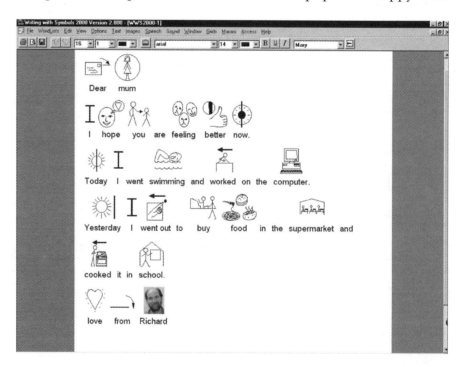

the e-mail message they have written, highlight all the text and symbols (click and drag with the mouse or press Ctrl A). Copy the text onto the clipboard by pressing CTRL C. Open your e-mail writer (Outlook Express, Eudora, etc.), click in the message box and press CTRL V. This will transfer the text of your symbol message only into the e-mail. Address and send the e-mail. Similarly when you receive

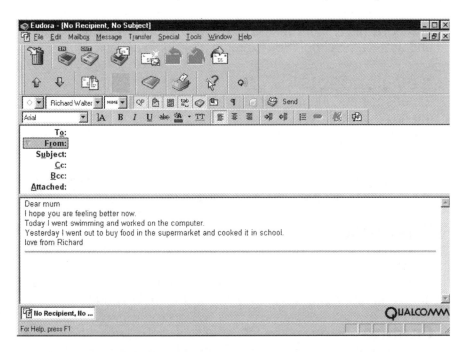

an e-mail you can highlight (CTRL A) and copy (CTRL C) the text from the e-mail program, open Writing with Symbols and paste the text in with CTRL V. This will then construct a symbolic version of the e-mail which can be spoken by the computer or printed out (you will probably need to alter and arrange some of the symbols according to your pupils' needs).

Using the Internet – pupils with profound and multiple learning difficulties

Many of the pupils at Meldreth Manor School have profound and multiple learning difficulties, some of whom will not be fully aware of the concepts of an audience but mainly attend to immediate experiences within their own experiences and understanding. They are mainly operating in the encounter phase of development, reacting, sometimes inconsistently, to obvious changes in their environment.

Using the Internet for browsing the web is difficult for these pupils due in part to some of the characteristics of the Web; it is generally a slow media, complex and difficult to navigate, which falls short of the full multimedia usually needed by these pupils for successful learning.

One of the possible uses of the Internet with pupils who have profound and multiple learning difficulties is in the creation of multimedia pages that can be used as web pages.

- Experiencing real objects connected with the activity.
- Using digital cameras to collect images and a sound recorder to record sounds of familiar activities.
- Making a multimedia presentation of these resources.
- Showing the presentation to an audience in school and to a wider audience outside school.

Making a multimedia record and webpages of a familiar area and activity in school. For example, the riding school.

Key concepts

Experience and identify sensations and objects associated with the riding school.
Experience and identify sounds associated with the riding school.
Recording sounds and pictures of the riding school.
Combining sounds, images, objects and sensory experiences into a multimedia presentation for the class.

Resources

The riding school, horses, and real objects from the riding school.
Digital camera, sound recorders, computer, multimedia authoring package, symbol processor, Internet connection.

Outline

Visiting the riding school, collecting real experiences of the facility.

Recording activities and events:
Collecting objects, exploring objects and showing them to the class.
Collecting sound recordings and playing them to the class.
Collecting images (digital photos) and showing them to the class.

Creating records of the riding school, tactile and sensory books, symbol writing, digital photographs, multimedia presentations.

Presentation to an audience in school, showing the records as sensory media and computer multimedia using the computer projector.
Presentation to an audience outside school using web-based multimedia.

The technique of recording immediate familiar environments and school events using real experiences, objects, sounds, images and creating a number of different records from these resources; object boxes, tactile books, multimedia and webpages, forms the basis of many ICT-related activities in school. It has formed the basis of the school web site.

The following is an example recording sheet that can be used to create multimedia records of activities and places in school. This can create a 'story board' to construct multimedia and webpages.

Multimedia/webpage recording template

Name _____ Date _____

Picture/Object

Symbols/Text

Sound/Video

In summary, we believe that many concepts involved in using and programming the Internet can be introduced to pupils with learning difficulties so long as they are securely rooted in concrete experience. Interestingly, we have found the same to be true of introducing these concepts to colleagues. Those attending courses have found these very practical exercises valuable in helping them to understand some of the more arcane aspects of using the Internet.

Chapter 4

Enabling access

In this chapter we will be looking at various ways of making web-pages more accessible to people who have difficulty in using the World Wide Web. We will consider:

- How webpages are normally accessed.
- How you can alter some of the settings in Windows to help access.
- How you can alter the settings in your own web browser to make webpages more accessible.
- How you can use alternative access devices (including the keyboard, overlay boards and switches) to access web pages.

Pages on the World Wide Web are normally accessed by using a mouse, pointing and clicking at links on the pages. These links can be text (which is usually highlighted in a different colour and/or underlined) or pictures which usually have a thin coloured border around them to show that they are links to other pages. There can be a number of links and they can be in any position on a page.

    The mouse pointer usually changes shape from the normal pointing arrow to a hand when it's directly over a link. By clicking on it, you will get transferred to that document, no matter where it is stored on the Internet.

Normal access

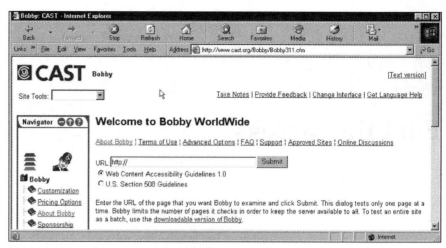

Figure 4.1 The cursor arrow. The pointer is not over any linked text, clicking the mouse button has no effect

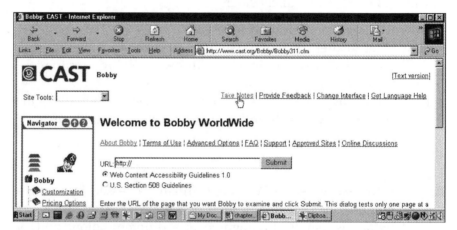

Figure 4.2 The pointer is over a link and becomes a pointing hand, clicking the mouse button moves to a new page

What happens when normal access to webpages breaks down?

There are several possible reasons why people can have difficulties accessing pages on the World Wide Web.

People with *visual difficulties* can have difficulty viewing pages, reading text and pictures and seeing the links between pages. Pages on the World Wide Web can be graphically very confusing, the text can be small and closely laid out and the use of graphic or patterned backgrounds can render the text very difficult to read. The linking text can be graphically very similar to normal text. The mouse pointer can be hard to see, particularly when there is a complex background.

People with *hearing difficulties* can have difficulty in hearing pages which have sound or music. The World Wide Web is still largely a visual medium but the use of sound integrated into webpages is increasing and some pages are now using sounds for navigation information.

People with *physical difficulties* may struggle to control a mouse and click mouse buttons. They may find it hard to have fine enough control to move the mouse so that the arrow is precisely over a link and remains there while the correct mouse button is clicked.

People with *cognitive difficulties* can have difficulty understanding and interpreting the information and in navigating the pages.

People with learning difficulties can find it difficult to process all the information on a page; they might find the page setup unclear. They may have problems discerning where the links are, they might have difficulty reading text and they also might have other related problems of coordination and visual difficulties.

1. You can alter some of the settings in your own browser so that it will display the webpages in ways that will enable better access to pages on the World Wide Web.
2. You can alter the settings within the Windows operating system to make the mouse easier to control, so that access to webpages is easier.

What you can do to make pages on the World Wide Web more accessible

For people with visual difficulties

There are a number of simple alterations you can make to your browser settings:

* You can alter the graphic layout (turn off the background graphics to have a plain contrasting background).
* You can change the background colour to enhance the text.
* You can increase the size of the text.
* You can change the colour of the links to make them stand out more.
* Individuals might find it easier to interpret simple text rather than a complex picture so you can turn off the graphics entirely.

For people with moderate visual difficulty

* You can alter the browser settings to enlarge the text and use additional access support software; for example a screen reader can be set up to read parts of a page.
* You can use a screen enlarger to increase the size of parts of the screen.
* You can add sound to links.
* You can use a speaking web browser.

For people with severe visual difficulty

* You can enhance the links with sounds.
* You can use a speaking web browser or additional speech programs to read a web page.
* You can provide direct keyboard access to links on the web pages.

Figure 4.3 summarises these methods.

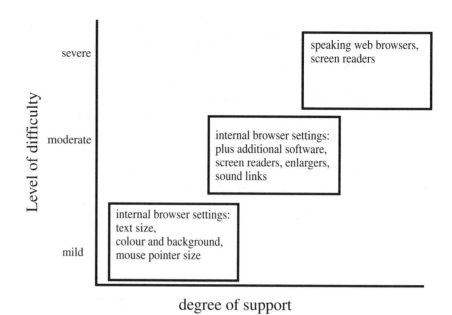

Figure 4.3 Enabling access for people with visual difficulties

Hearing impairment

The Web is still largely a visual media. Sound is not often very important and is seldom essential for navigating pages. If the web page has been written to include meaningful alternative text labels (see Chapter 5 on writing accessible websites) and descriptive text transcripts of sound files, you can use these text links instead of relying on sound for meaning.

Physical difficulties

People who have physical difficulties can find it difficult to move a mouse precisely so the mouse arrow is over a link and then to use the mouse buttons to click on a link.

For mild difficulty

- You can alter the browser settings to enhance the clarity of links by changing the colour and size of the text links.
- You can alter the mouse settings on the computer: slowing down the rate of movement, adding a trail to the mouse arrow, and altering the click acceptance rate so clicking is easier.

For moderate difficulty

- You can change the browser and the mouse control settings and use alternative input devices.
- You can use alternative mice, which might be easier, or roller balls, joysticks or a graphic pad instead of the standard mice.

For severe difficulty

- You can use a keyboard, overlay board or switches to access pages.
- Direct keyboard, overlay board or switch access, scanning access to links.

Figure 4.4 summarises these methods.

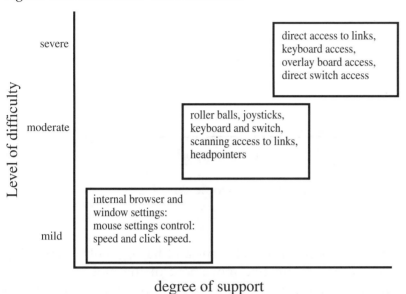

degree of support

Figure 4.4 Enabling physical access for people with visual difficulties

Cognitive difficulty

People who have a cognitive difficulty (learning difficulties) probably have difficulty understanding the information on the webpages. They will probably have a degree of physical impairment and perhaps some visual and/or hearing problems too.

For mild cognitive difficulties

- You can alter the browser setting, making the pages clear and uncluttered; you can alter mouse settings to make the mouse and pointer easier to use.

For moderate cognitive difficulties

- You can alter the browser settings and use additional software to enhance links using speech and sound navigation aids.
- You can use different mice, a roller ball, joysticks.

For severe cognitive difficulties

- You can use the keyboard, overlay board or switches to access the links on a page.
- You can use the keyboard, overlay board or switches to access whole pages (in a page turning slideshow).

Figure 4.5 summarises these methods.

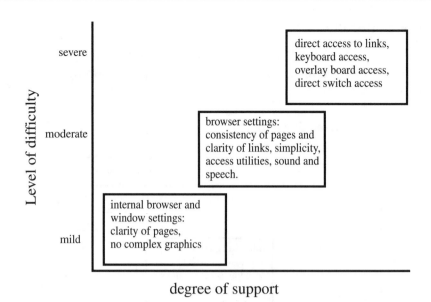

Figure 4.5 Enabling access fo people with learning difficulties

Case studies Peter has a slight visual impairment and has difficulty controlling the mouse, especially in fine movement of the mouse arrow. We therefore used a large arrow for the mouse pointer. We altered the mouse characteristics in the control panel, slowing down the mouse movement and adding a mouse trail. We additionally made both mouse switches act as the select button.

Sam has severe physical difficulties such that he cannot use a mouse. He used a headpointer to control the mouse arrow with the dwell facility to activate a link. We increased the size of the text and the links on some pages in our browser setup.

Hina has visual difficulties and severe learning difficulties. Access was via a mixture of keyboard, touchscreen, overlay board and switches.

Access difficulty	Problems	Possible solutions	Additional solutions
Visual impairment	Difficulties viewing pages, text and pictures. Difficulties in using a mouse to navigate pages	*Windows setup:* Enlarge mouse pointer, add mouse trail, slow mouse movement *Browser setup:* Enlarge text, turn off background colour	You can use screen readers or browsers that support speech output and Braille
Physical	Difficulties in controlling the mouse and clicking on links	*Windows setup:* Alter mouse settings *Browser setup:* Enlarge text, turn off background colour	You can use additional input devices: roller balls, keyboard, overlay board and switch access
Cognitive	Difficulties in understanding page layouts. Difficulties in controlling mouse	*Windows setup:* Alter mouse settings *Browser setup:* Enlarge text, turn off background colour	

Table 4.1 Summary of access difficulties and possible solutions

There are also a number of modifications you can make to the Windows operating system, especially to improve access for people who have difficulty using a mouse. The mouse setup can be found within Windows setting control panel accessible from the Start menu (Figue 4.6).

How to modify the Windows setup to enable better access to an Internet browser

Figure 4.6 By clicking on the picture of the mouse in the control panel you can modify the size of the mouse arrow and how the mouse behaves, its rate of movement and the speed at which it accepts a double click

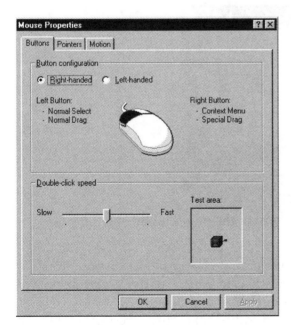

Figure 4.7 Changing the mouse settings in Buttons

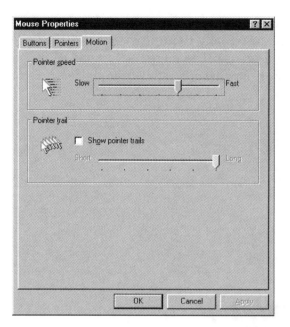

Figure 4.8 Changing the mouse settings in Motion

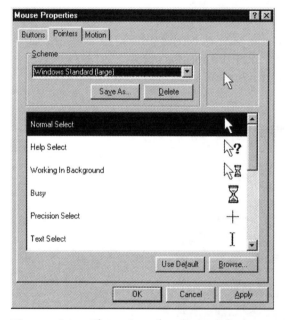

Figure 4.9 Changing the size of the mouse pointer

You can get a number of larger and clearer mouse cursors from the Ace centre web site (www.ace-centre.org) that you can download and install on your computer.

You can also further use an additional mouse access program such as Toggle Mouse (www.toggle.com) to enlarge the mouse pointer, make both mouse buttons operate as one and have a finer control over the speed and movement of the mouse arrow (see Figure 4.10).

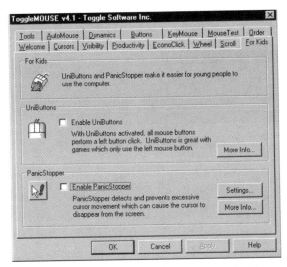

Figure 4.10 The Toggle Mouse control panel

You can alter some of the settings on your browser so that it displays any pages on the World Wide Web the way that best suits your access needs. This can be done with most web browsers, for example, in

- Internet Explorer
- Netscape
- Opera.

How to modify some settings within your own browser to enable better access

Changing the display using Internet Explorer

First you need to allow your browser to use its own settings when you are viewing pages. Bring up the Internet Options settings by clicking on Tools on the top menu bar (see Figure 4.11).

Figure 4.11

In the Tools menu choose the internet options (Figure 4.12):

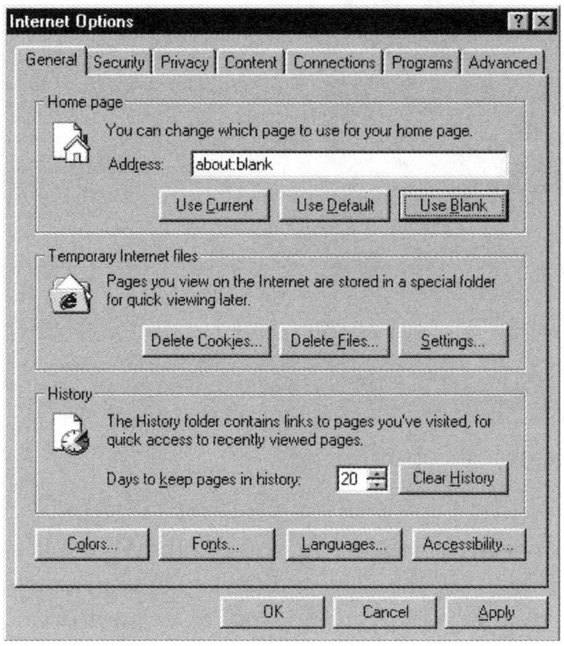

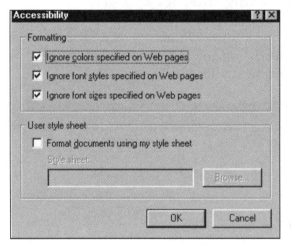

Figure 4.12

Click on the Accessibility tab and change the format to ignore the settings specified in the web pages (Figure 4.13):

(Click on OK)

Figure 4.13

Then click on the Color tab and change the background and the font colours to plain and contrasting colours: 'for example' black text on light yellow (Figure 4.14).

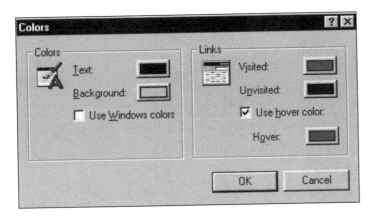

Figure 4.14

Click on the Font tab to change the type of font that is used in your browser to display the pages (for maximum clarity a non-seriffed font is recommended) (Figure 4.15):

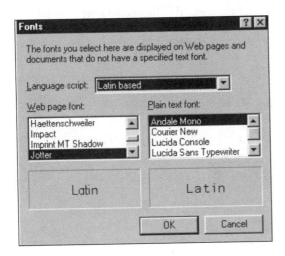

Figure 4.15

You can also change the size of the fonts that are displayed on your browser:

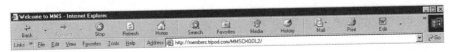

Figure 4.16

Click on View in the top menu bar and choose Text size:

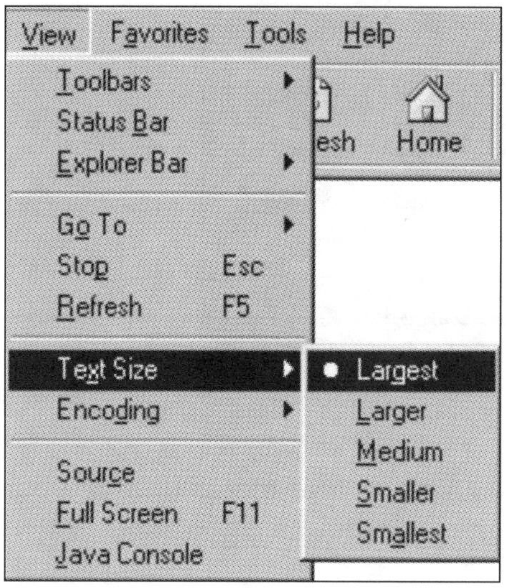

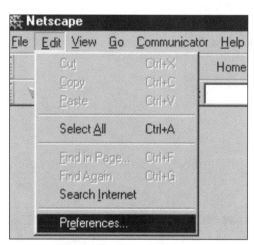

Figure 4.17   Altering the size of the text displayed when you view Webpages

How to alter the settings in the web browser 'Netscape'

Choose the Edit menu and then choose Preferences (Figure 4.18):

Figure 4.18

In the preferences you can alter the size and type of the font
(Figure 4.19):

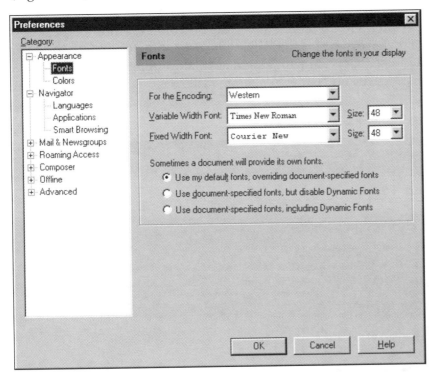

Figure 4.19

You can choose the screen colours displayed on the webpages
(Figure 4.20):

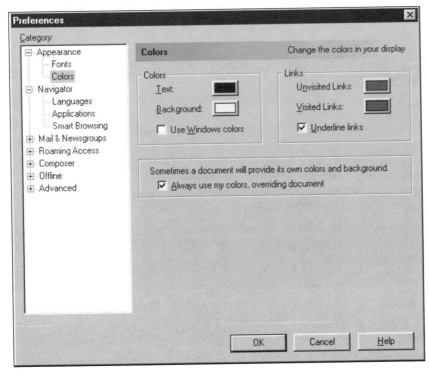

Figure 4.20

How to change the accessibility options in the web browser 'Opera'

While Internet Explorer and Netscape account for most of the access tools that are used for the Web, there are estimates that up to 10 per cent of users operate with Opera as it takes up only a small amount of disk space and claims to operate faster.

Click on File from the menu bar:

Figure 4.21

and click on preferences

Figure 4.22

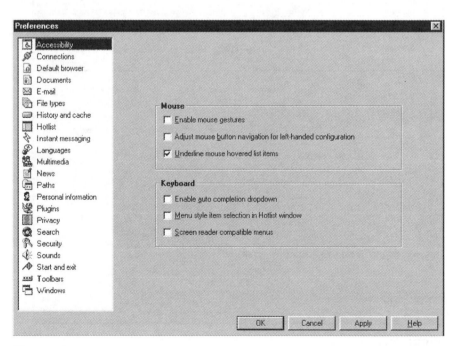

Figure 4.23

Click on Documents to alter the text sizes, the background colour, and the link presentation.

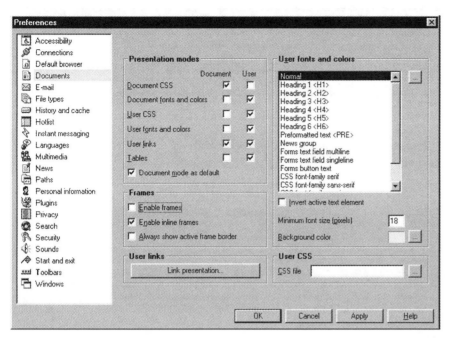

Figure 4.24

The effect of changing some of these settings can be dramatic, enabling access to pages that might be incomprehensible to certain users. The following is an example of how changing some browser settings can help to make pages more accessible (Figures 4.25, 4.26, 4.27).

Starting with a graphically very cluttered page:

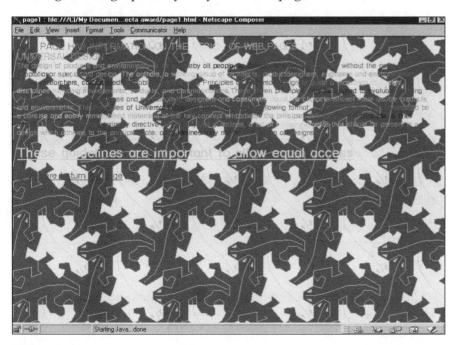

Figure 4.25

1. The effect of turning off the background graphics, selecting a neutral background colour with black text:

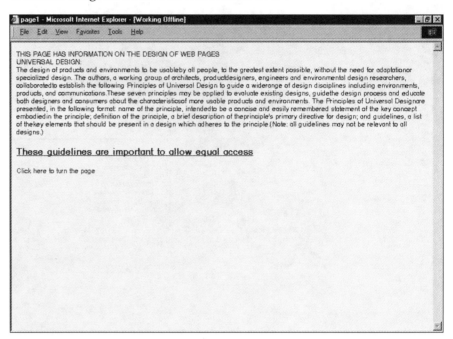

Figure 4.26

2. Increasing the size of the text:

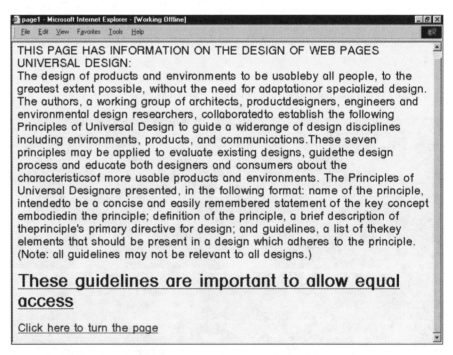

Figure 4.27

However, even with these modifications, there will be a number of people who cannot use a mouse or pointing device to access webpages. For these individuals you will have to investigate using various additional access devices to enable access to the World Wide Web.

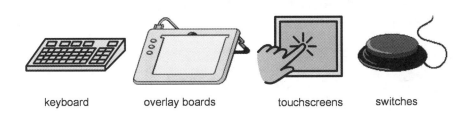

keyboard   overlay boards   touchscreens   switches

Stepping forwards and backwards between pages

Perhaps the simplest way to view pages on the Web is stepping forwards and backwards between whole pages. Web pages which have already been visited by your computer on the World Wide Web are stored in a special folder on your computer so that they can be viewed quickly without fetching them afresh each time from the Internet. They can be stepped forwards and backwards from the toolbar by clicking on the arrows on the browsers toolbar with any mouse button or by using additional mouse switches.

Figure 4.28   The backwards and forwards arrows in Internet Explorer

Figure 4.29   The backwards and forwards arrows in Netscape

Figure 4.30   The backwards and forwards arrows in Opera

The keyboard can also be used to move forwards and backwards between pages.

Using Internet Explorer, Netscape Navigator or Opera you can go forward and backwards through pages using the ALT arrows keys (holding down the Alt key and pressing a forward or backwards arrow key). Alt-right arrow turns to the next page (similar to clicking on the toolbar Forward button). Alt-left arrow turns to the previous page (similar to clicking on the toolbar Back arrow).

If your mouse software driver allows you to assign different functions to Buttons (such as the Microsoft intellimouse) then in Mouse Properties in the Windows setup control panel you can alter the Buttons, assigning one button to step forward through pages.

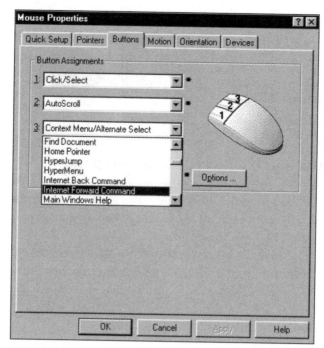

Figure 4.31

With any overlay board (Concept keyboard, Intellikeys board, Discovery board, etc.) you can program the board to send Alt-left and Alt-right arrow. You can program two cells, one to be Alt-right arrow, the other Alt-left arrow to navigate through pages on your computer. For example, using the Intellikeys board:

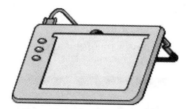

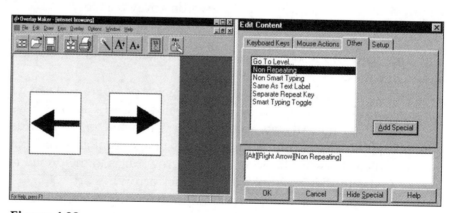

Figure 4.32

Program the overlay with two cells, one to move forwards through the webpages (sending Alt-right arrow), one to move back (Alt-left arrow).

Using Overlay boards to access whole pages

You can create overlays that let students go directly to websites when they press an area of the overlay board.

You can program individual cells with a full Web address (URL) of a page (for example www.meldrethmanor.com) which will take you to that page on the World Wide Web. You can have writing, symbols or a graphics on the paper overlay.

Run Overlay maker and start a new overlay by clicking on New in the file menu (or by clicking on the new page icon, see Figure 4.33).

Access to whole pages on the Web using the Intellikeys board

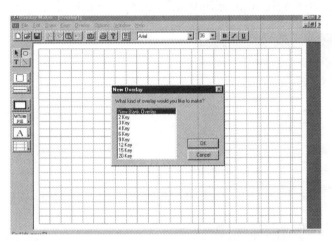

Figure 4.33

Choose an overlay size (here I have chosen a 6 key layout)

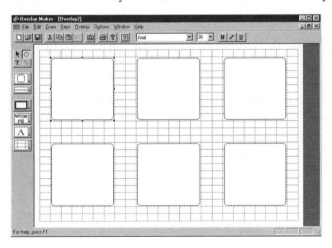

Figure 4.34

To create an overlay that will open webpages in Internet Explorer or Netscape Navigator you have to program a cell or area on the overlay board:

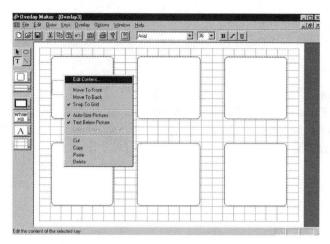

Figure 4.35

Click on a cell with the right mouse button and choose Edit Content:

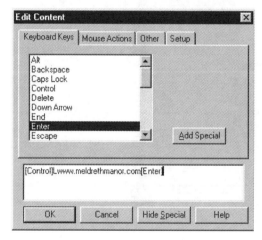

Figure 4.36

Put in the following codes:

1. Choose Control from the keyboard keys menu then click on Add Special.
2. Type in the letter L.
3. Type in the web address of the site you want to visit (or you can copy and paste from the address line or from the links or favourites lists of your browser).
4. Choose Enter from the Keyboard Keys menu and click on Add Special.

The key content should be in the format:

[Control]L   (this opens a new window in your internet browser)

followed by the web address (URL) of the site (for example www.meldrethmanor.com)

followed by [Enter]

This works with both Internet Explorer and Netscape Navigator.

To do a similar overlay with the web browser Opera you need to put the following into the key content:

[F8]www.meldrethmanor.com[Enter] changing the 'Control L' to 'F8'

Next choose pictures and text to create the paper overlay, for example:

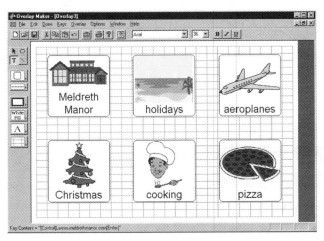

Figure 4.37

then click on Send Overlay (see Figure 4.38):

Figure 4.38

Click on Print to make the paper overlay that is placed on the overlay board. Your overlay board then will be ready to be used. Pressing an area on the Intellikeys board will open your chosen web page.

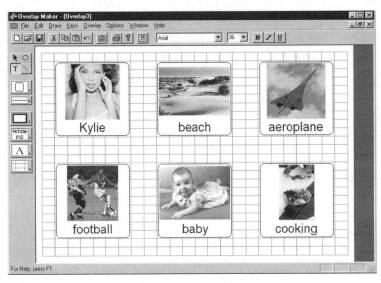

Figure 4.39 An example of an overlay made using pictures taken from websites.

Using the Intellikeys board you can further control pages on websites by using the switches that can be attached to the overlay board to send a page forward (alt-right arrow) and a page backwards (alt-left arrow).

Click on Overlay in the menu bar and then Switch 1:

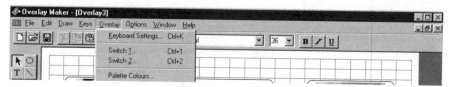

Figure 4.40

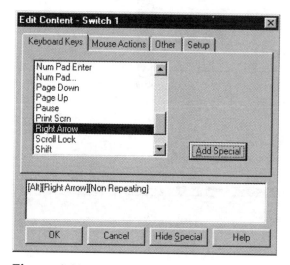

Figure 4.41

Switch 1 will then turn the next whole webpage. Similarly set Switch 2 to act as a back arrow by sending [Alt][Left Arrow][Non Repeating] You then can use the overlay to choose sites and the additional switches to step forwards and backwards between pages.

Access to whole pages on the Web using the concept keyboard

The following method of using the concept keyboard has been provided by Sally Paveley of the Advisory unit (www.advisory-unit.org.uk) and included with her permission.

- Run your browser, e.g. Internet Explorer.
- Run Concept Plus Editor and drag out an area for your first web link.
- Type a name, e.g. Eastenders, into the Enter text for overlay box.
- Use the Graphics button to add a graphic if you want one on your printed overlay (you could get this from the website but you will have to save it as a bitmap).
- Now display your browser.

- Go to the website you want to link to.
- Highlight the address line (www. etc.) by clicking in it.
- Hold down the Ctrl key on your keyboard and press C. This will copy the address to your clipboard.
- Display Concept Editor again.
- Click the Send tab.
- Click the Keys button.
- Choose Alt from the list of keys.
- Click in the When chosen send box and type FO on your keyboard.
- Hold down the Ctrl key on your keyboard and press V. This will copy the address in your clipboard.
- Click the Keys button again and choose Enter.
- Now click OK.
- Repeat for more web links.
- Save and print when you have finished.
- To use your overlay:
  Run your browser and Concept Plus
  Choose your overlay file from the Concept Plus file menu
  Display your browser
  Press the Concept Keyboard to go to a website.

All these techniques access whole webpages which have already been stored in your computer's memory by visiting the pages of the site on the Internet (this is known as offline browsing). You would have had to visit every page of a website if you wanted to switch through the whole site using these simple page turning controls.

There are, however, some very useful utilities that will download the whole of a website onto your computer so that you can step though it even when you are offline (not connected to the Internet). Webcopier ,WebReaper, WebZip and WebWhacker are all programs that allow you to download a complete website onto your computer. All the pages can then be accessed using these simple page forwards and backwards commands.

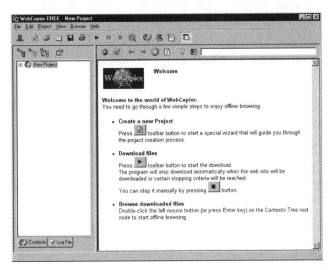

Figure 4.42   The front page of WebCopier, an offline browser that records and stores websites on your computer (www.maximumsoft.com)

Using these techniques you can record and store complete websites on a computer, these can then be used as classroom resources, accessed via a network or transferred by writing onto a CD-ROM.

All these methods are limited to accessing complete webpages in a kind of slide show. To access individual links within the page you are going to have to use some different techniques.

How to access individual hyperlinks within a webpage using the keyboard

You can access the individual links in a webpage by using the tab and return keys from the keyboard in Internet Explorer to step through the links, or by using the CTRL-up and CTRL-down in Opera; enter or space will then access the chosen link. These can be made accessible to overlay board users by programming a cell with a tab character, and one with 'Return'. However the highlighting of the links in web browsers is generally very poor, limited to drawing a narrow outline around the linked text or picture.

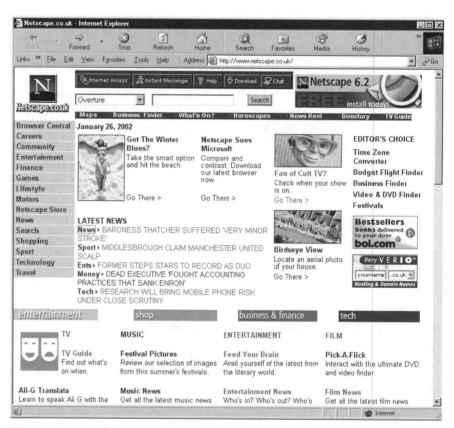

Figure 4.43   The tabbed focus is on News, pressing the enter key will load the News page.

There might be hundreds of links on a page, some might be graphics and some text, and they can be irregularly placed all over the page. The sequence in which links are activated by the Tab key can also be irregular so that the highlight box may jump around all over the page.

For these reasons tabbing between links is not really a good method of accessing graphical links in complex webpages. (It is however useful when used in combination with a screen reader for people with visual difficulties.) Any indirect access method such as switch or keyboard stepping through links on a webpage requires considerable cognitive and physical abilities.

(In chapter 5 we will describe how to change the sequence that links are stepped through if you are creating your own pages on the World Wide Web.)

How to connect switches to access links in webpages

To connect exterior switches to control scanning through links you will need a way of sending the tab and return keys using switches, you can do this using a number of switch interfaces.

Figure 4.44a

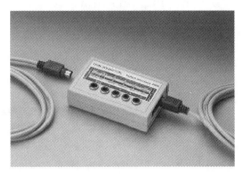

Figure 4.44b

Most switch interfaces will allow switches to act as tab and return.

You can also use switches connected to the Intellikeys board to switch through the links and access the links with switches.

Start Overlaymaker and set up Switch 1 to send 'tab' and Switch 2 to send 'enter':

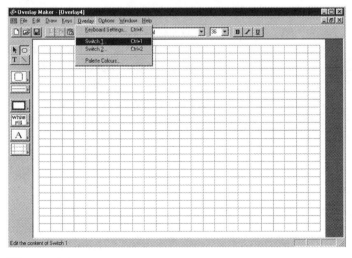

Figure 4.45

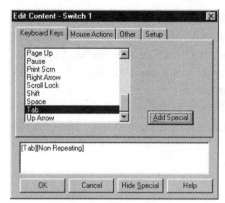 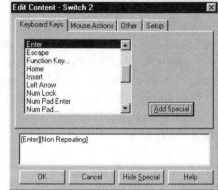

Figure 4.46a   **Figure 4.46b**

On webpages switch 1 will step through the links and switch 2 will activate the highlighted link.

The highlighting of active links in web browsers is so poor that this method of tabbing between links is really only useful for people with specific difficulties (for example a visual impairment and they are using a screen reader).

How to get direct keyboard or switch access to links on webpages

People with severe physical and cognitive impairments often find it easier to control pages directly, connecting a switch or a keyboard input to directly control a link rather than using two different keys to scan through the links.

Using a hotspots program

To set direct access to links on a webpage you are going to have to use additional access programs that can create 'hotspots' areas on the page that can be activated from the keyboard. These can then be accessed by the keyboard, overlay board or switches.

You can use Clickit (Inclusive technology), Hotspots (Ace centre) or the Discovery switch (Don Johnson) to get keyboard/switch access directly to positions or hotspots on the screen. You could then access pages without having to have previously visited and downloaded every page. However, on most pages on the Web the links are irregularly positioned so you would need to adapt each page to make the links into hotspots. Adapting each page for direct access could be extremely time consuming and not really worthwhile for general Web browsing.

The technique of adding keyboard hotspots to a page only works well on webpages if they have a consistently placed navigation controls, for example forward arrows, on each page. It is not recommended for using in general Web browsing.

Figure 4.47 An example webpage that has been designed to be easily used with supplementary access programs and devices

Voice navigation

These are systems which allow voice-driven navigation of webpages, some with both voice-in and voice-out, and some allowing telephone-based Web access.

One of the more interesting recent developments in access technology has been the advent of continuous speech recognition as a means of accessing the Web. The latest versions of Dragons' Naturally Speaking software and IBM's Via Voice both offer the potential for hands-free access to a computer. Of the two, Dragons software is probably the easiest to use, but requires a computer with a good quality soundcard, 800mHz processor and 256MB of memory to be entirely reliable.

The voice models utilised by the software are now created far more rapidly, and can offer 95 per cent reliability after only 40 minutes training. But they do require a degree of consistency in the speech of the user and the ability to remember sequences of instructions and a number of discreet commands. However, in a number of cases they have been extremely useful in offering access to the Web, e-mail and other applications where physical access is either impossible or extremely uncomfortable or painful.

Matching access technology to individual needs is a complex process. Much more information on many of the above can be found at www.abilitynet.co.uk and where access requires a degree of fine tuning it may be that individual assessment and advice either from the ICT coordinator, SENCO, LEA advisor or an external service such as AbilityNet, ACE centres or Cenmac may be appropriate.

Conversa Web is a voice-activated browser allowing spoken selection of links using 'saycons'.

Access	Mouse	Keyboard	Overlay board	Switches	Comments
To complete pages	Click on the forward and backwards arrows on the browser toolbar	Netscape and Internet Explorer: ALT+Left ALT+Right arrow keys Opera: Z or CTRL+Left or ALT+Left X or CTRL+Right or Alt+Right	Overlay board programmed to send the correct keystrokes (ALT+Left) and (ALT+Right)	Switches send correct keystrokes (ALT+Left) (ALT+Right)	The browser needs to have visited and download all the pages off the Internet first
To links within pages	Click on the text or graphic links	Internet Explorer and Netscape: Tab steps through links, return activities link Opera: Q or CTRL+Up, A or CTRL+Down space/return activities link	Overlay board programmed to send the correct keystrokes: Tab and return	Switches set up send the correct keystrokes: Tab and return	The highlighting of links on browser pages is usually very poor. There can be any number of links positioned anywhere on a webpage

Table 4.2   Access summary

In Chapter 5 we will discuss methods of writing webpages which enable access utilities to function easily and we will look at some additional access programs (using additional Javascript) that you can easily add when creating your own pages on the World Wide Web.

Designing accessible webpages

Chapter 4 discussed some adaptations you can make to the Windows operating system or to the way your browser displays webpages to enable better access to web pages. Chapter 6 discusses what should go into your webpages. This chapter will consider how you construct the actual pages and then how you get them onto the World Wide Web. We will explore how access can be enhanced by thinking about key issues in writing the code and designing pages on the World Wide Web.

This is not a full tutorial on how to code webpages in HTML but it will consider some of the design principles to aid accessibility and will outline some of the tools you can use to create an accessible website. There are a number of very good tutorials on the Internet on creating accessible web pages, for example at http://www.w3schools.com/.

To create your own pages on the Web you need:

- a computer with an Internet connection;
- some space on the World Wide Web to store your pages;
- a way of loading your pages onto your web space;
- a way of creating the HTML web code for your webpages;
- content to put into your webpages.

Tools to write webpages

Internet connection

You can get free Internet connections from most of the Internet service providers (ISPs), for example Freeserve, Tesconet, Btclick. Many of these ISPs also come with some free web space.

Web space

The web space given to you is stored on the Internet service provider's server and can be accessed from anywhere on the Internet.

FTP (file transfer protocol)

To load your finished pages onto the Internet you will need an FTP program to transfer the files from your computer onto the Internet service provider's server. Many ISPs who provide some free web space also supply a program to upload your webpages onto the Internet.

Figure 5.1 is an example of a file transfer program to load your pages onto your web server.

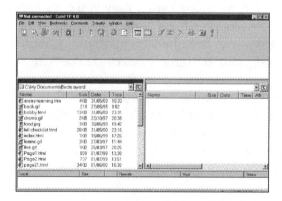

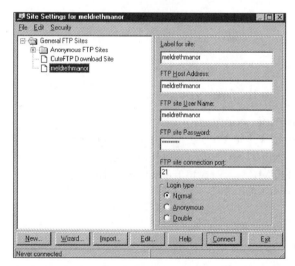

Figure 5.1 Creating the code for web pages

There are many free FTP programs that you can use including SmartFTP, FreeFTP and AceFTP

Once your pages are successfully transferred onto your Internet provider's server they can be accessed from anywhere on the World Wide Web.

When viewing a webpage, if you click on View and then on Source from the menu bar of your browser you will see the HTML coding for that webpage.

Pages on the World Wide Web are written in HTML (HyperText Markup Language). This is a universal code understood by all the different computers on the Internet. HTML is a developing programming language, the latest version (as of February 2002) is HTML version 4.01 which is also known as XHTML v1.

HTML 4 extends the old HTML with mechanisms for style sheets, scripting, frames, embedding objects, improved support for right to left and mixed direction text, richer tables, and enhancements to forms, and offering improved accessibility for people with disabilities.

In order to make your own web pages you need some way of creating this code (HTML).

At the simplest level, if you write a page in a desktop publisher like Microsoft Word you can simply save it as a webpage. Choose the option from the File menu to 'save as' a web page. This will save the page in a format that can be used in a web browser on the World Wide Web. It will save your Word file in two parts: the HTML file (which is a text file) and any pictures in a separate folder. Several word processors and desktop publishers can save documents as webpages. This is generally fine for simple pages, or for transferring a single document or article onto the Web, but for a website which is more complex, with linked pages, it is not powerful enough.

Some providers offer integrated utilities to make designing your first pages easy. An ISP such as CompuServe will provide Homepage Wizard with a range of templates for your first site, and a web space provider such as Tripod may also offer a 'Studio' to help you with your first efforts online.

To create more complex linked pages it is better to use a dedicated HTML editing program. These allow you to insert images, create links and manage your web site. There are several different examples of these. On the Windows platform there are Front Page, 1st Page 2000, Hot Metal Pro, Hot Dog Pro, Incontext Spider, HTML Assistant Pro and many more. In addition, there are fully professional products such as Dreamweaver from Macromedia which offer still further advanced features to a budding webmaster. These dedicated editors offer a number of additional features to help you construct your website and they can also check your HTML for errors or accessibility features.

To view pages from the World Wide Web on your computer you need a 'web browser'. This is a software program which interprets the text, pictures, sounds and multimedia from the Internet and lays them out as pages on your computer screen. The two most well-known web browsers are Internet Explorer and Netscape. However, there are

71

many others; Opera, Lynx, Mosaic, etc. Earlier in this book we explained how to modify some settings on these browsers and the Windows operating system to make all webpages appear more accessible.

The beginning

Here is an example of a very simple web page:

```
<TITLE>This is my first web page</TITLE>
<BODY>
<H1>This is my first web page.</H1>
</BODY>
```

which is shown by the web browser as Figure 5.2.

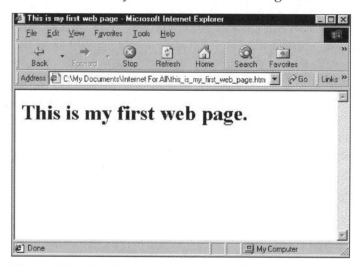

Figure 5.2   Beginning to create a web page

There is a fundamentally important difference between webpages and pages written in a desktop publisher and word processor. When you write pages on a desktop publisher you place text, specify its size and font on your page and you can place pictures on your pages precisely. Web pages, however, are simply written as a series of text instructions that are interpreted by your computer's web browser to display the webpages.

HTML is not a Page Description Language for doing DTP work: it does offer a degree of control over the final page appearance, but can never give total control. It should never be used to specify the exact layout of pages.

Another difference between word processor files and webpages is that there is an international Standards Committee for HTML: it is the World Wide Web Consortium (W3C) at CERN in Geneva.

There are lots of different types of word processor files (for example Microsoft Word and Lotus Works save their text in completely different formats) and different word processors have difficulty in reading each other's files. Webpages, since they are written to a universal standard, should be able to be viewed on any computer (or any Internet device) using any web browser. They need not (will not) be shown in exactly the same way but they should all operate successfully or 'Degrade gracefully'. This is what is known as the universality of the World Wide Web.

The result of all this is that it shouldn't matter which computer nor which browser is being used to browse the World Wide Web. The same webpage can be shown as simple text, braille, speech, or as a full multimedia format. It also means that you can alter the settings in your browser so that the webpage can be viewed in the format that is most accessible to you or your pupils.

Guidelines for writing accessible webpages

If you are in the position of creating your website there are guidelines you should follow to ensure that your own pages are as accessible as possible or can be used easily by supplementary access programs. The universal guidelines www.design.ncsu.edu:8120/cud/univ_design/princ_overview.htm provide a framework for the basic principles for creating all accessible software including webpages.

Principles of accessible software

1. **Choice of input methods**
    Support the user's choice of input methods including keyboard, mouse, voice and assistive devices. The primary requirement is to provide keyboard access (mouseless operation) to all features and functions of the software application. The operating system usually provides support for input via the serial port, keyboard movement of the mouse pointer, and other keyboard enhancements.
2. **Choice of output methods**
    Support the user's choice of output methods including display, sound and print. The primary requirement is to provide text labels for icons, graphics and user interface elements and to support visual indications for sounds. Implementing the accessibility APIs (e.g. Java Accessibility, Microsoft Active Accessibility, etc.) for the target platform will meet this principle.
3. **Consistency and flexibility**
    Make the application consistent with the user's choice of system behaviour, colours, font sizes and keyboard settings. Provide a user interface that can be customised to accommodate the user's needs and preferences including fonts, colours and display layout.

There are a number of guidelines specifically about creating webpages from the W3C.

W3C offer ten key tips for website design, which are an extremely useful guide for schools:

- **Images and animations**. Use the **alt** attribute to describe the function of each visual.
- **Image maps**. Use the client-side map and text for hotspots.
- **Multimedia**. Provide captioning and transcripts of audio, and descriptions of video.
- **Hypertext links**. Use text that makes sense when read out of context. For example, avoid 'click here'.
- **Page organisation**. Use headings, lists, and consistent structure. Use **CSS** for layout and style where possible.
- **Graphs and charts**. Summarise or use the **longdesc** attribute.
- **Scripts, applets, and plug-ins**. Provide alternative content in case active features are inaccessible or unsupported.
- **Frames**. Use the **noframes** element and meaningful titles.
- **Tables**. Make line-by-line reading sensible. Summarise.
- **Check your work**. Validate. Use tools, checklist, and guidelines at http://www.w3.org/TR/WCAG.

The W3C has a great deal of information on how to write accessible websites. Their recommendations are organised into three levels of priority. Each checkpoint has a priority level assigned by the Working Group based on the checkpoint's impact on accessibility.

Priority 1
A Web content developer must satisfy this checkpoint. Otherwise, one or more groups will find it impossible to access information in the document. Satisfying this checkpoint is a basic requirement for some groups to be able to use Web documents.

Priority 2
A Web content developer should satisfy this checkpoint. Otherwise, one or more groups will find it difficult to access information in the document. Satisfying this checkpoint will remove significant barriers to accessing Web documents.

Priority 3
A Web content developer may address this checkpoint. Otherwise, one or more groups will find it somewhat difficult to access information in the document. Satisfying this checkpoint will improve access to Web documents.

For example, providing alternative texts for all graphic images is priority 1 while not using blinking text is priority level 2.

The priority levels for different features of webpage design can be found on the W3C website:

http://www.w3.org/TR/WAI-WEBCONTENT/
http://www.washington.edu/doit/
http://trace.wisc.edu/world/web/
http://www.cast.org/bobby/

What to avoid when creating your website and examples of some bad webpages

There are a large number of poorly written websites on the World Wide Web, many of them produced by major corporations!

Some of the things to avoid in constructing a website are:

- ugly and intrusive backgrounds;
- unreadable text, clashing background colours or images;
- very large graphics (try to keep them between 10k and15k);
- including a large number of graphics on a page;
- scrolling banners;
- lots of animated icons and animated graphics;
- large background music files;
- blinking text;
- pages that only work at one resolution;
- improper use of frames and using too many frames;
- large blocks of text;
- scrolling text;
- too many links on a page.

You can further explore badly designed webpages at http://www.webpagesthatsuck.com/

In Chapter 4 we saw that there is a certain amount of alteration you can do to your web browser's settings to make pages appear more accessible. This is generally limited to removing confusing backgrounds, graphics and making all the text larger.

The major way to ensure that your own website is accessible is at the design and coding stage. If you want to make your site especially accessible to one particular group of users then other issues will need to be considered but a well designed website will be more accessible to a wider audience. At Meldreth Manor School a great deal of care was put into designing part of the site for switch users. The further guidelines we used when constructing the Meldreth switch accessible site were:

1. Consistent, clear layout of pages.
2. Plain backgrounds and clear links.
3. Pages to fit on a single screen without scrolling.
4. All graphics to have good alt text labels.
5. Pages to be optimised for fast downloading.
6. Text to be simple and short.
7. Symbol support for plain text.
8. Extra access utilities easily available.
9. Page turning controls consistently placed on every page.

The way in which the pages are written can make huge differences in the accessibility of a site to any viewer on the World Wide Web. As an example we can look at a hypothetical design of a webpage:

Figure 5.3

This page is graphically very confusing, unreadable and unclear as to what to do

We can rewrite the page:

1.   Remove confusing background images (Figure 5.4).

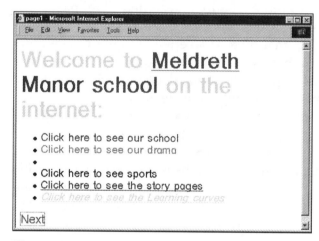

Figure 5.4

2.   Remove multicoloured text (Figure 5.5).

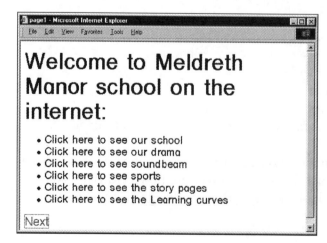

Figure 5.5

3. Separate and emphasise the links adding a plain background colour and pictures (Figure 5.6).

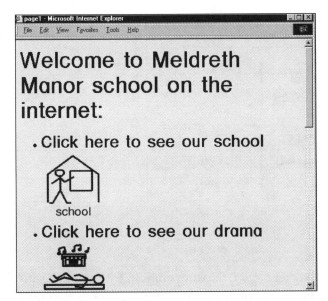

Figure 5.6

4. Alter the layout to make the page fit one screen (Figure 5.7).

Figure 5.7

5. Further emphasise the links and place consistent page controls (Figure 5.8).

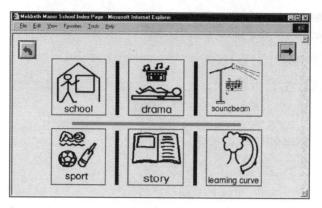

Figure 5.8

The Meldreth website

As we explained in Chapter 6 on 'Choosing content for your website' we decided in planning the Meldreth site that to make it totally inclusive it would be easier to divide into different areas:

- A text and information site containing text pages about the school, about the curriculum, its planning and implementation, information for teachers and parents on ICT and our pupils.
- Help pages on how the site is laid out, how to use the Web with some ideas and utilities to enable access to pupils.
- A switch accessible site. These pages were developed to be accessible to all pupils using additional overlay board and switches and useable with any browser. They were developed from pupils' experiences in school and designed to be as accessible as possible to the majority of pupils.

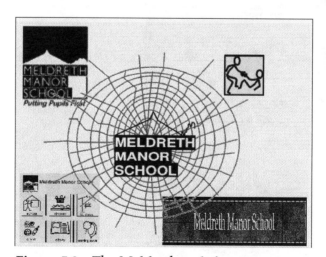

Figure 5.9   The Meldreth web front page

We can see how all these design principles are applied by looking at two linked pages from the Meldreth switch accessible website (see Figure 5.10).

Figure 5.10

Features are:

- plain backgrounds with a large single centralised image;
- simple symbol supported text;
- every page fits within a single screen (17-inch monitor) without the need for scrolling;
- consistently placed links in the same position on every page;
- keyboard control of page turning (using the Accesskey coding and some Javascript (see below)).

A consistently placed 'next page' arrow has been included so that leaving the mouse pointer in one place will allow users to navigate by using supplementary mouse switches.

The only position on a webpage where you can guarantee that links will be in the same position on every page is at the very top of the page (there are specific commands in HTML to specify left, middle and right) so a consistently placed link has to be positioned at the top of each page.

Some pages include a sound effect that enhances and annotates the browsing for individuals.

Additional scripts and controls you can use to assist access to Webpages

In HTML 4.0 there is a facility in the HTML script to provide direct keyboard activation using the accesskey markup:
<a accesskey='key' href='url'>name of link</A>

for example:

<a accesskey='a' href='index.html'>Back to the index page</A>

The 'a' key on the keyboard when used in conjunction with the Alt key would activate the link to the index page. To make these links switch-accessible you will need a switch interface that will map a keystroke to a switch.

Organisation and links

Consistent design reminds visitors that they are visiting a complete site and not just a jumbled collection of pages. When using links avoid using 'click here' but explain exactly what happens if you click on a link. Consider how beneficial banner ads really are to your site.

1. Is there a link back to the home page on each of your webpages?
2. Are navigation links positioned in the same place on each page?
3. Is the website layout logical and intuitive?
4. If you use frames, have you titled each one?

Technical considerations

As you design your website consider whether you need to use plug ins, scripts and applets. If you can, consider offering a non-frames version of your site. If you have Java-enriched pages, can the site sill function if the Java is turned off?

1. If you display your site in a low screen resolution 640×480, can you still see the text?
2. If you switch off the graphics in your browser can you still understand your pages?
3. Have you tested your website against one of the Accessibility services?

The Meldreth web pages include coding for the accesskey so that the linked page turning arrow can be accessed directly from the keyboard. Every page includes the code:

```
<A ACCESSKEY="1"HREF="next_page.html"><IMG SRC="right.gif"
ALT="Next     page"     WIDTH=40     HEIGHT=40     ALIGN
="RIGHT"></A>
```

This allows the page turning arrow to be directly accessible from the keyboard. The keystroke that is linked to the page turning arrow depends on the computer system being used. For instance on machines running MS Windows one generally has to press the ALT key in addition to the access key, so in the above example you would use ALT key in addition to the access key (Alt 1).

You can easily set up any overlayboard to send an ALT keystroke. Switches could either be set up with the Intellikeys board, Windows switch or the programmable switch interface from Inclusive technology.

Using extra JavaScript to enhance access

JavaScript is an additional scripting language that is interpreted by your browser and allows simple programming.

Mouseover control

Some of our pupils can control the mouse arrow but they find it difficult to move the mouse pointer over a link and then click a mouse button in the link. There is a very short simple JavaScript code that you can add to any text or graphic link.

When the mouse arrow is moved over the yellow arrow button the link is activated and next page is loaded. Using the Mouseover script, a link can be activated by moving the mouse pointer over an area of the screen, without the need for clicking the left mouse button. The JavaScript you need to add to your HTML script for a mouseover control is:

<AHREF="nextpage.html"ONMOUSEOVER="parent.location="
nextpage.html"> < IMG SRC ="rightarrow.gif"ALT ="next page"
WIDTH ="40" HEIGHT ="40" ALIGN ="LEFT"></A>

where "nextpage.html" is the name of the page you want to link to and "rightarrow.gif" is the picture link you want to use.

An example of using this JavaScript mouseover can be seen on the switch accessible site of the Meldreth webpage (see Figures 5.11 and 5.12).

Figure 5.11

Figure 5.12

The yellow arrow is activated by a 'mouseover'. This alternates position on every other page (since a static mouseover link in the same position on every page would not pause once a page was loaded). The blue arrow is still the consistently placed switch-accessible link.

Autoscroll

People who cannot exert fine control of the mouse will find it impossible to scroll down a page so every page has to fit on a single screen. Using JavaScript you can make a page scroll automatically. The following script can be cut and pasted from a supplier such as www. bigscripts.com into your web page to achieve this result.

```
<script language="JavaScript1.2">
/*
Advanced window scroller script-
By Website Abstraction (www.wsabstract.com)
Over 200+ free JavaScripts here!
*/

var currentpos=0,alt=1,curpos1=0,curpos2=-1
function initialize(){
startit()
}
function scrollwindow(){
if (document.all)
temp=document.body.scrollTop
else
temp=window.pageYOffset
if (alt==0)
alt=1
else
alt=0
if (alt==0)
curpos1=temp
else
curpos2=temp
if (curpos1!=curpos2){
if (document.all)
currentpos=document.body.scrollTop+1
else
currentpos=window.pageYOffset+1
window.scroll(0,currentpos)
}
else{
currentpos=0
window.scroll(0,currentpos)
}
}
function startit(){
setInterval("scrollwindow()",10)
}
window.onload=initialize
</script>
```

Timed page turning
Including a timed link using JavaScript can act as an automatic page turn prompt to anyone viewing the web pages:

```
<SCRIPT LANGUAGE="Javascript">
<!—setTimeout("top.location.href='nextpage.html'",30000);//—
></SCRIPT>
```

where "nextpage.html" is the page you want to link to.

This would automatically activate the link to the next page after 30 seconds. If the page turning also activates a sound this can be quite useful. The Web is designed to be an interactive media and removing control from the user should be considered carefully.

Link listing
You can use a JavaScript program to list all the links on a web page and assign a keyboard letter to each link so the keyboard can be used to access the links directly on a web page.

Examples of these JavaScript scripts (and many more) can be found on the web at:
www.bigscripts.com, www.java-scripts.net and www.thefreesite.com

Inclusive planning in practice

There are government recommendations for the creation of official government department web pages. These can be found on:
http://www.cita.gov.uk/iagc/rtfs/websites.rtf

We can look at some of the key points of this document as a good example of clear guidance.

Homepage, navigation and display

Government sites should have clear navigation which is easy to use. Navigation has often been overlooked by designers in favour of the look of the site. Information and services on websites are only useful if customers can find them. The recommendations in this section aim to ensure that the user can navigate the website using whatever technology is available to them.

Departmental web teams should ensure that:

• the homepage is found at the URL that is served as the homepage by the server (i.e. www.name.gov.uk not www.name.gov.uk/namehome.html);
• there is a link to the homepage from every page;
• the main navigation menu is available from the homepage;
• the main sections of the website should be accessible within one click from the homepage;
• the logo of the department or organisation is included on each page.

83

Frames should only be used where there is no straightforward alternative for navigation. If frames are implemented then a 'No frames' alternative must be supplied for the entire site and access to it should be easily visible on the homepage with a link in or near the top left corner to assist those using Access Technology. If frames must be used, extensive testing must be undertaken to ensure that 'nesting' only occurs when it has been specifically programmed. When frames are used, descriptive labels should be utilised (e.g. 'Navigation Bar').

If menus are designed using non-HTML techniques, e.g. JavaScript or Shockwave, an alternative menu must be supplied using standard HTML.

Text and graphic links

Not all users choose to view websites using graphics, and many are unable to use images at all. These individuals may be using small-screen browsers which only display text, or may be blind users with Access Technology.

- Where graphics are used for linking, a text alternative must be included.
- ALT tags must be used with images, even if an alternative text link is present.
- Imagemap navigation methods should be used sparingly. Where it is used, a text alternative must be supplied. Imagemaps must have ALT tags for each menu option.
- JavaScript mouse and roll overs must not be relied upon for the provision of core information or navigation options.
- Text-based menu bars are more helpful to users of Access Technology when menu items are split with the bar (|) character. This avoids any problems with the Access Technology reading all the links as one – where the designer feels that the bar character is unappealing, it can be in the same font colour as that of the background, thus not appearing to most users.

Tables

Tables can create difficulties in some browsers, and particularly for users of Access Technology. It is unreasonable to insist on a no-tables policy for all government websites but designers must be aware of the problems that can arise, and consider how their sites perform with Access Technology.

- The number of columns used should be kept to a minimum.
- Where tables are used to present content in multiple columns designed to be read horizontally, BETSIE or a similar system must be implemented.
- Nested tables are best avoided and only used where there is no alternative.

- Tables are rendered differently by different web browsers and must be checked for compatibility.
- The Cols attribute must be included in the Table tag.
- If a fixed width table is used it must never exceed 600 pixels.
- Ending tags must never be omitted.
- Background images in tables should be avoided as they are not supported by older browsers.
- Background colours are not supported by older web browsers.

Graphics – ALT tags

ALT tags are essential for those users who do not or cannot view images. They are also useful for search engine positioning.

- The website should be useable with the graphics turned off.
- The ALT tag must be descriptive.
- The ALT tag must not exceed 100 characters.
- ALT tags must always be included in imagemaps.
- It is recommended that where an important logo is used for the first time (for example on a homepage), a full and official description should be given (such as "X Department Logo: Coat of Arms featuring…" etc.). When the logo is then repeated, it can be referred to in the ALT text as "X Department Logo").

Testing for accessibility

The site may be tested using Bobby (www.cast.org/bobby/) or a similar system. Although this is an automated system, it can provide helpful results.

The site should, where possible, be tested using Access Technology; alternately, the RNIB (www.rnib.org.uk) can audit sites.

ALT tags must sufficiently replace the information supplied by the graphics used.

File naming conventions

The following file naming conventions, which are HTML best practice, are desirable to assist continuity of approach for the benefit of those joining established web teams.

- File names should be in lower case. This lessens the likelihood of broken links or images.
- There should not be gaps in file names.
- Where file names are split, the underscore (_) character should be used.
- No other forms of punctuation should be used in a file name.
- File names should not exceed 50 characters.

- File names should be descriptive.
- HTML file extensions (e.g. htm/html/shtml) must be specified and adhered to.

File sizes

Large files are expensive and time consuming to download, especially for those with slow modems. This is exacerbated if, as is the case for small businesses, sessions are likely to be during the period of peak call charges. Large homepages have the added disadvantage that the user cannot choose a more economical means of accessing the site.

Different types of web page require different file size restrictions, thus:

- Homepage total file size should not exceed 30k.
- Standard, informational page total file size should not exceed 120k.
- Special case pages (such as reports, statistical data etc. where it is advantageous for the user to be able to print the file in one job) total file size should not exceed 300k. In such cases, the user should be warned in advance of the file size. Good internal navigation is also required.

Colours – palettes

The 256 colour web palette should be used for hyperlinks and text. Original graphics, where possible, should be generated using the web palette, excluding JPEG images.

Background colours should be selected from the web palette. Background colours must contrast with text colours. Avoid using red and green together (these are the colours which pose most common problems for colour-blind users).

Summary

In this chapter we have attempted to highlight a number of the key issues in designing your own web pages, so that they are accessible to people with a disability. Entitlement is a key issue in developing inclusive practice, and the school should bear these guidelines in mind, not just when designing a school website, but for any intranet or pupil-accessible site within the school.

Chapter 6

Choosing content for your website

Having decided to create a website for a school, individual or whoever, one needs to decide what the intended audience will be. This is harder than it sounds. As we designed the sites for our own school, so the audience changed. Initially we wanted a site for our own school to access, then parents, then friends and the wider family, then other teachers, and finally anyone who wanted to.

We wanted a site that celebrated our achievements, that provided high levels of access, that was interactive and fun to visit. We did not want an electronic prospectus. We had seen many of these on the Web and thought they were boring. We also wanted to write sites that anyone with minimal knowledge of coding could learn from. While Richard had talent and could code in HTML, David wanted an easy option with nothing more complex than copy and paste!

To meet all of these requirements we broke the site into a number of sections for its content. In practice these became the headings for our navigation tree:

- *Our work*. A celebration of the achievements of the pupils at the school.
- *Our interests*. Anything we wanted to put on the Web that we thought others might want to see.
- *Our news*. Latest updates on what was happening at the school.
- *Our games*. Puzzles, interactive elements, arcade games to encourage people to come back and visit again.
- *Our services*. Anything that we could offer visitors for free, this included software we had created, a fantasy shop, electronic postcards, horoscopes, etc.
- *Contact us*. A range of ways in which visitors to the site could interact with staff and pupils from the school.

In each of these a lot of planning and thinking had to be done to create the resources needed. We chose to host the multimedia site on a free provider of webspace, Tripod, as they offered the service for free and plenty of space of which we could make good use.

Our work

Pages in this area were often linked to areas of the curriculum that pupils were taking part in. One page had copies of poems written in symbols, another had examples of art work. Figure 6.1 shows part of the result.

Figure 6.1   A 'contents' page for the various displays of work

Displaying art work is one of the easier examples of page design. The pupils had been using great artists as an inspiration and we took their creations and set them as the background of a blank page. These looked especially attractive when displayed on the screen (see Figure 6.2).

Figure 6.2   An example from Arts4all

Activities that pupils took part in could be photographed. This was made easier by the purchase of digital cameras that could save images in .jpg format. Photos were taken of science experiments, and most successfully of a day trip to Calais, here described in rebus symbols by the pupils concerned (see Figure 6.3).

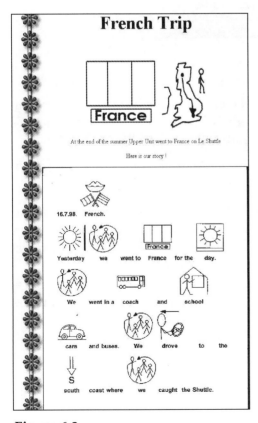

Figure 6.3

Having taken part in a number of music and dance events, we were then able to place streaming video into the site to report on activities. While quality was still a little slow, the technology was improving all the time. Video of pupils performing with Soundbeam with a range of professional musicians remains some of the most viewed content on our site (see Figure 6.4).

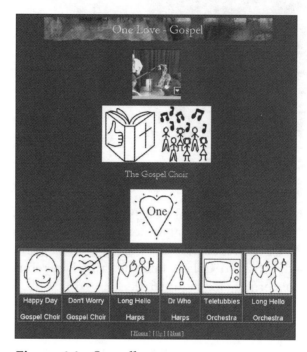

Figure 6.4 Soundbeam page

In celebrating pupils' achievements all aspects of technology can be brought together to create an electronic board that emphasises high expectations and success rather than disability.

Our interests

Some of the pages we designed made pupils talk about related things of interest. Most especially, pupils wanted to talk about their hobbies and things they did in their leisure time. Some of the most popular pages were about music, TV and animals.

To augment their pages pupils worked with images of the Spice Girls as a collage for one page and others found links to EastEnders sites. Another group thought up some questions for comedians Stewart Lee, Richard Herring and Kevin Eldon which went into an interview (see Figure 6.5). What should not be surprising was that the areas that the pupils wanted to write about were the same as for pupils without disabilities. As Martin explained – 'I want to write about Leicester City not wheelchairs!'

Kevin Eldon Interview

Pics from TMWRNJ thanks to Rob Sedgebeer

The Actor/Comedian Kevin Eldon agreed to give us an interview in June 99

It took us six months to send him the questions

He answered within 24 hours

Thanks Kevin

KE   Hi everybody,

Thanks for your questions and I hope you're all well and happy

MMS   What was the best and worst things about school for you?

KE   Best things at school: girls, three card brag round the back of the R.E. hut, school plays, mucking about, latin and french, really good laughs with all my mates, bag of chips at dinner time.

Worst things bullies (they only do it cos they were bullied themselves. Stop the bullies I say. There's no such thing as ratting on a bully. If you tell someone in charge what's going on you're doing a great job for everybody else who's getting bullied.)

Some of our teachers were bullies. Hope there are none at Meldreth Manor School. If there are everybody get together and jolly well dunk his/her horrid head into a large vat of lumpy custard in the canteen kitchen.

Figure 6.5   The Kevin Eldon interview

Our news Like most schools we published a newsletter for parents and friends on a regular basis. The aim of the news pages was to add news more often, in a multimedia format and in accessible ways. The school paper newsletter is scanned and can be downloaded from the site as well as being part of an archive of news.

The use of video and digital images enhances these pages considerably. Any school event, Christmas, fete, or trips out can be reported on here. The news page is divided into months and each month is updated regularly.

This was one of the first pages which we developed with the use of Java scripts and Java Applets. These two features allowed us to make better use of our space and to add animations and interactive elements to the page. The first script we added was a Java Applet that created an up-to-date school diary for parents and visitors to use. An ISP provided this free. Secondly we added a small script that allowed photographs to be displayed as a slideshow. This was especially successful in displaying images of fireworks that we had taken at the school display each year.

We also grew this section of the site by adding a collection of scanned press cuttings. The school had attracted a lot of local and national press coverage for its work with technology and we were able to keep an archive online of all that had been said about us in this way.

We further extended this section by adding a page of views from others. Interesting visitors to the school, from a Talk Radio producer to the local Bishop, were asked to write a few words about their thoughts and perceptions of seeing us at work to be shared with visitors to the site. Figure 6.6 is an example of a views page.

Figure 6.6   Example of a views page

As we created the site we realised that we needed to offer visitors as much to do as possible. This promoted the idea of the site as interactive and followed a school philosophy of making resources available to the community. Our first pages of games were very simply adapted graphics – a spot the ball game, with the ball bouncing during parachute games, photo clues of places we had visited around the world ranging from Warwick Castle to Rhodes.

As time progressed we wanted to take this still a stage further. A trawl of the Web found Connie King's Loonyverse site and she kindly allowed us to use her games and applets to enhance our own. One of the most pleasant things about the Web is the spirit of mutuality and sharing that still exists.

Our games

The spirit of mutuality has pervaded much of the development of the Web. Examples that have impacted upon each of us have included those who give up free time to moderate discussion groups and often, in practical terms, free advice that is given when one posts a question on an intractable problem. Looking back over the past two or three years, we would estimate that we have saved hundreds of pounds by using the free advice offered on the Internet rather than taking our computers to a workshop for new software drivers to be found and installed.

When we found people to help us, some of our pupils wanted to help others. We agreed that we should offer copies of simple switch software that they had made with teachers and we chose to create a fantasy shop where others could practise making purchases online. Using resources made available for free we were able to set up a daily cartoon/joke service and a daily horoscope. The value of these lay in pupils helping to select the services we would offer and the self esteem that grew by doing something for others.

Our services

Many of the staff at the school had e-mail addresses and we used a free provider of e-mail (Hotmail) to provide still more. We felt, however, that this was only one form of contact and we wanted to add others. Again the notion of interaction and sharing was key to our design. We used a number of free services to add these elements to our site.

We chose to add a Guest book where visitors to the site could make their comments about what they liked about the site and what they didn't. We added a mailing list so that visitors would be automatically sent a newsletter, and could e-mail other members of the list. We then added a chat room which was used for an online 'chat' Question and Answer session between the head teacher and a small group of parents. We then added discussion forums in which threads of discussion points could be followed through by visitors and users of the site.

Contact us

The outcome of these initiatives was that the site felt increasingly like a meaningful link between the school and the community, both that of friends and families, those living locally to the school and ultimately those who were part of a wider community of people with disabilities.

Single issue sites

Any of the areas above could be expanded as the sole content for a site, examining one single issue and pursuing it in greater depth than is relevant to a broader site. Areas that have been particularly successful for schools from the mainstream have included sites about our environment. The best known of these is the 'Mission Possible' site by Sutton Park School in Dublin (see Figure 6.7). This site explored issues around the protection of the environment through an interactive game that one played online. A huge range of excellent examples of sites for and by children can be found at the Childnet International website (www.childnet-int.org). Other examples are shown in Figures 6.8 and 6.9.

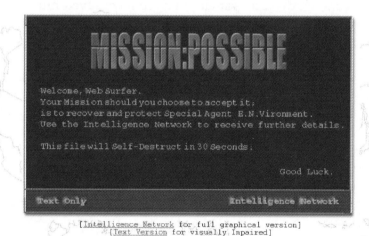

Figure 6.7 Mission Possible – Environmental site, Sutton Park School, Ireland

Figure 6.8 Children's folk games – Collections and survey –
Duiliu School, Romania

Figure 6.9 Casa Alianza – Street Kids speak out – Costa Rica

Looking at the types of articles pupils produce for school
magazines it is easy to see how a school could have a site of celebrity
interviews, arts galleries or pictures of pets, etc. These could be
expanded to establish links with other schools and hence to create an
online community with shared interests.

Ultimately, it is down to the imagination of the creators to decide
what content they want to have online.

Summary

The selection of content for a school or personal website is extremely important. In selecting our content we thought carefully about what made us go back to websites after a cursory visit, and then again about what was the philosophy behind the creation of our website.

Valuable sites for online resources

www.tripod.com
A free webspace provider, but which offers users much more in return for embedded advertising. We were able to make use of guestbooks, horoscopes, newflashes, CGI scripts and Java all provided by Tripod for free. We do recommend them.

www.thefreesite.com
Lists of links to free resources. These include Java script and Java Applets. If you don't know where to start in adding elements to your site then this is the place to start.

www.loonyverse.com
Lots of free games and graphics, including all of the Java and Shockwave games displayed on the site.

www.ice-network.com
Source of our online calendar.

www.listbot.com
Will set up a free mailing list for you.

www.bravenet.com
A huge range of free services including counters, guestbooks, discussion forums, etc.

Chapter 7

Resources on the Web

In looking to review the availability of a range of resources we have focused on a number of criteria. The resources we have recommended have all been available at these addresses for the past year, they are all available free of charge and they have all been recommended to us by people with disabilities or professionals working in the field, as offering quality of information or service. The list is by no means exhaustive but we hope it offers a useful starting point and benchmark for you to use.

There are many websites that have been established to support teachers in working with children with a disability. In reviewing the opportunities that are available, one needs to take into account the dynamic nature of the Web which evolves and changes on a daily basis. As a result this review is based upon services and interactive provision on the Web rather than specific sites and resources that are available.

Searching for resources

As with much on the Web, this is not quite as easy as it sounds. In thinking about this question we would offer the following as useful search terms when seeking further and more recent sites:

General disability and technology issues: Disability + technology; Disability + computer; Disability + adaptive technology; Disability + Access+ technology.

Visual impairment: Visual loss; Blind.

Physical disability: Cerebral palsy; Motor impairment; Physical handicap.

Hardware: Use: Assistive technology / Adaptive technology, + disability + country you wish to search in.

Special education – pan-disability groups

There are a number of common issues that link together much of the work that is done within special education and with people with a disability more generally. Here we have referred to these as 'pan-disability'. Such organisations may cover aspects of provision to people with special needs as a part of their work, or they may be focused on one aspect with a wide range of people with disabilities. One aspect of pan-disability sites that may be of value to those searching for support is that they are often larger organisations and may be funded through statutory sources.

BECTA (www.becta.org.uk)

The British Educational Communications and Technology Agency offers a wide range of resources to professionals working in the field of disability. Most especially, they maintain a fully searchable database of reviewed resources to support inclusion. A range of fact sheets and updates on educational resources are regularly available for download. The site also hosts what is probably the largest set of discussion forums for educators in the UK as well as links to all of the major listservs.

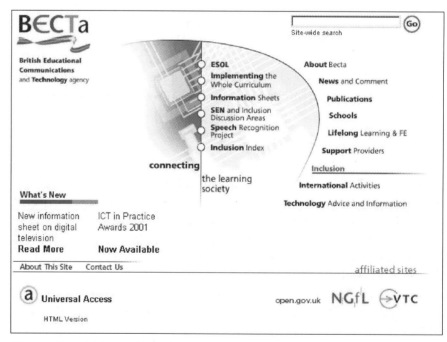

Figure 7.1 A BECTA web page

NASEN (www.nasen.org.uk)

The National Association for Special Educational Needs is a UK organisation publishing useful information about access and the teaching of people with a disability. The website provides details of publications and a useful set of links to online resources.

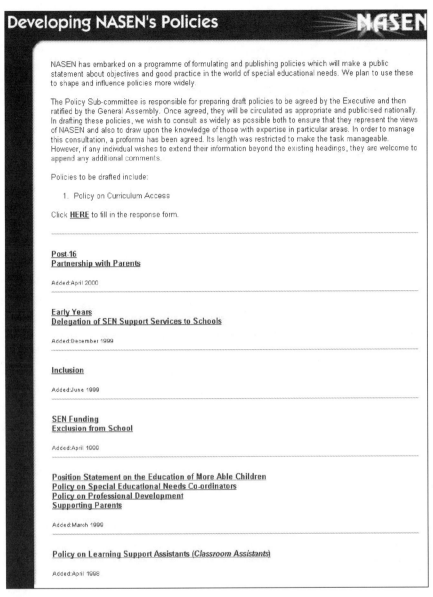

Figure 7.2   NASEN web page

As can be seen from Figure 7.2 a particularly useful aspect of the site is draft policy on a range of SEN issues that are helpful in stimulating discussion and debate within schools.

CSIE (http://inclusion.uwe.ac.uk/csie/csiehome.htm)

The Centre for Studies in Inclusive Education is an example of a single issue pan-disability group on the Web. CSIE focuses upon how schools and education systems can include all children with a disability into the mainstream classroom. As such it can be an invaluable source of information to teachers and managers working to promote inclusion. Figure 7.3 gives an example.

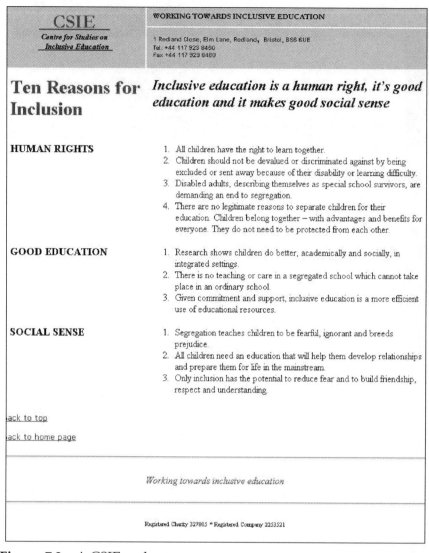

Figure 7.3 A CSIE web page

A site such as this illustrates a key point that is worth considering. There is no obligation upon any site manager to offer a balanced view of any issue that it discusses. As with most research it is important to encourage staff to look at issues from more than one point of view by visiting a range of sites. Not all sites will be as clear as the CSIE in identifying their political position as soon as you visit.

Disability resources and groups

Many of the major disability groups have developed specific sites to assist in the provision and dissemination of information. These vary hugely in quality and value but can broadly be categorised as those that deal with a variety of disabilities, and those which deal with a single disability. An example of a cross-disability site would be that of the charity AbilityNet which deals with the provision of information relating to a wide variety of needs, but only in the area of access to technology (www.abilitynet.co.uk). Alternatively, a site such as that of the Royal National Institute for the Blind (www.rnib.org.uk) will provide a wider variety of information on a greater variety of topics but will only look at the needs of those people with a visual disability. Most search engines will help you find the URL of such a group if you search for the name of the charity or the disability. When making such searches it is also useful to add the country to your search terms if you want to narrow the information to that of your own locality.

Some of these information sites can also provide assistance in a different form. For instance the AbilityNet site can provide you with a link to a freephone line, assessment services and supply of equipment. In these cases the website can offer a starting point for a wider search, or it can be a one-stop shop if the services offered are those required.

One of the best sites that we have found for free resources on the web is www.thefreesite.com (Figure 7.4). None of the resources is specifically educational. But if you want to add free elements to your site to make it more interesting then this is a very good start. It was through this site that we discovered bravenet.com who can offer free hosting for all the interactive elements you may want on your site. These can include guest books, forums, chat rooms, mailing lists, etc.

We also found thefreesite.com to be a good and well maintained set of links to free code for JavaScript or Java applets to spice up your site, and there were many links to free graphics materials including backgrounds, arrows, buttons, etc. If you are a webmaster then you may well be able to use resources designed to look pretty as useful educational tools. For instance, on one visit to the site we found a range of simply animated graphics designed to fill a window in the browser. These proved to be ideal for encouraging some children with attention difficulties or a visual impairment to focus on the browser window as a precursor to accessing other types of information.

Among other resources that we found was Connie King's www.loonyverse.co.uk. Connie offers a range of materials that you can use on your site and a number of our online games were offered by her, as was the range of season-specific graphics that children chose from to make special Christmas or Halloween pages.

All of these sites are well worth a visit. Once such resources are available, teachers can concentrate on the important task of involving children in choosing from available resources and not spending long periods creating the resources from the beginning.

Support to webmasters

101

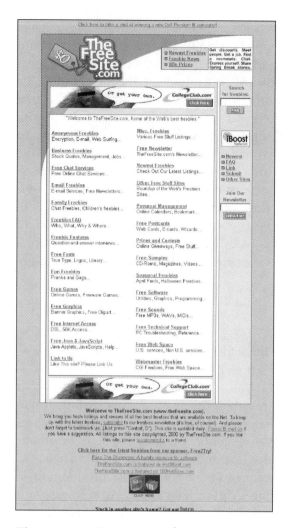

Figure 7.4   From www.thefreesite.com

Quality links   One of the problems in searching for information on the Internet is that there can be far too much information to deal with. One way to cope with this is to make use of one of the many links pages available on the Web. Basically, links pages are lists of useful sites that someone has taken the time and trouble to look at on your behalf. The best of these also offers a brief summary of the content of the site to assist you in determining whether this is a site that you would find useful.

To start with we recommend using www.independentliving.org. This site makes a good attempt to classify its links and is both nationally and internationally ranging. For a more focused directory listing we would recommend http://uk.dir.yahoo.com/Education/ Special_Education/ (see Figure 7.5). One of the useful features of such a site is the opportunity for people using the site to add their own links to a core list. Services such as Bravenet discussed earlier will host a set of user created links for you that do not require the webmaster to be involved in updating the links.

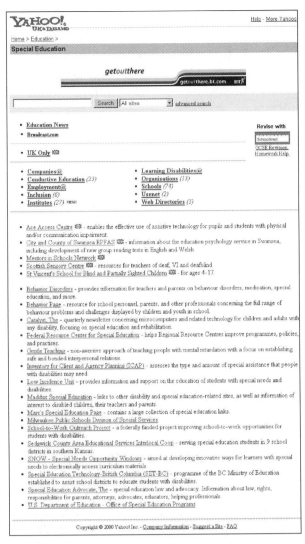

Figure 7.5 Yahoo disability links

As well as the useful links on thefreesite.com there are a number of sites that will offer free downloads of a range of pieces of software that teachers may find useful. One of the most longstanding of these is www.tucows.com, and we have found www.downloads.com to carry a very wide range of free and shareware software including web utilities. Among other utilities we have found on these sites there have been alternative pointers and carats, screen readers, and speech engines. All of these have real practical functions in supporting children with disabilities.

Teachers will also regularly find educational software at Beta or shareware stages of development. This allows teachers to investigate a piece of software before they try it, and moreover in the case of beta-test software to offer an opinion to the author before it is offered on sale. Examples of number and spelling programs can be found on either site.

Software support

103

Disability portals

Over the past year a number of disability portals have been established as gateways to the Web for people with a disability or professionals involved in disability issues. These are often a valuable source of news and information. Two of the best known are www.4dp.com and www.youreable.com; both contain access to news, products and information services.

Figure 7.6   4dp.com portal

Figure 7.7   youreable.com portal

Bobby

Bobby operates in two ways. The full service comes in the form of a freely downloadable piece of software that will allow you to gauge your webpage for accessibility. The program examines your source code and by applying the types of rules we have discussed earlier in this book, identifies the problems that the current set up would provide for a person with a disability. You can download Bobby from www.cast.org. There is in addition an online version of Bobby available from the same address which will give you instant feedback on any URL that you submit.

For sites that meet the standards demanded, the 'Bobby Approved' icon (see above) identifies the organisation as one that is committed to inclusion and accessibility. The Cast site offers a useful database of 'Bobby Approved' sites that recognises the efforts of webmasters and, in addition, publicises sites that could become a model for others who are interested in designing accessible websites.

Throughout the Web there are numerous pages offering details of the latest information on promoting access to technology.

Listservs

We have earlier talked about establishing a listserv of your own, or joining a listserv within your community. There are a great many listservs which interested professionals can join to access information and to ask questions of peers nationally and internationally and some of the links pages identified earlier will provide you with details of a range of listservs which you may find useful. As we have mentioned earlier one of these can be found at the Becta homepage, www.becta.org.uk.

The Web is a rich source of information and resources to help support the needs of people, including children, with a disability. However, finding resources can be a time-consuming process and the ability to make use of the experience of others in searching and investigating the opportunities is an invaluable time saver.

Once members of a staff team have identified their own favourite sites they can use a school intranet such as that discussed in Chapter 8 on staff support to share these throughout the school.

If you would like to share links without adding all the other aspects of an intranet then sites such as www.blink.com allow groups of users to post all their bookmarks onto a central server for named others to have access to. Again this can help with what is otherwise a technical task.

Connecting and supporting staff through the Internet

Since the publication of the first edition of this book, the business model upon which many of the services outlined were based changed radically; most are still available but not as free services funded through advertising. Instead they are usually now funded through a monthly payment, either as a block payment or as a monthly subscription. This subscription may vary according to the number of users who will be using the service with you. Wherever possible we have now outlined the business model for each of the services we have used.

In addition we have throughout used servicers that utilise the Web as the engine to connect people. Alternatives that can be used include establishing one's own server and having dial in connections. But in this case we are seeking solutions that require only limited technical expertise and little or no capital outlay.

In using the Internet with pupils with special needs, it is useful also to consider the range of ways in which staff can be supported through electronic communication. One of the greatest disadvantages of the break-up of LEAs over the past ten years was the loss of a number of means of networking with other teachers. While we are not claiming that the Internet can ever replace the face to face contact that took place, it does offer an opportunity to network on a local or national level.

One of the most useful means is e-mail. Every member of staff should be given an e-mail address of their own. A free e-mail address can be made available through hotmail.com or yahoo.com or many other free providers. Even for staff who do not have access to a computer at home, a web-based address such as this can be used from school, or at a cyber café or through the recently introduced web phones that can be found in public locations. Hotmail (free funded through advertising) also provides each user with a .Net passport from MSN. This allows the same username/password combination to be used across all the .Net services.

An example of the usefulness of this is the situation where a teacher is absent from work through illness. It may be quite possible for the teacher to e-mail lesson plans or notes into the school, reducing the problems for the school as a whole. This is a relatively simple approach; further opportunities arise if the school creates a web-based intranet, protected by a password, that staff can access both from school or from home. The creation of such an intranet need not be a complex process, and there are a variety of companies looking to host and create such sites for schools at low cost. One we have used is Intranets.com (monthly subscription). In discussing the opportunities created we shall draw upon the experience of using this site.

Web-based intranets

After completing a simple application form for intranets.com the site is created automatically. One can customise it with the school logo and set colours and newsletters which are automatically delivered to the site. The structure of the site is easy to navigate and it contains a number of simple sections:

Group calendar
Documents
E-mail list
Group contacts
Links
News.

Each of these can be used to support staff and attempt to reduce bureaucratic overload.

Group calendar

A regularly updated and maintained school diary is an essential element of a well run school. It can also be one of the more difficult things to achieve in a busy school. A group calendar on the Internet allows any member of staff to publicise an event in which they are involved – from a whole-staff meeting to the dates of the school Nativity play. Not only can the dates be quickly changed without

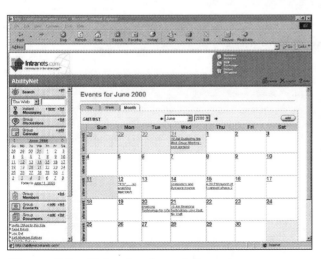

Figure 8.1   Calendar from intranets.com

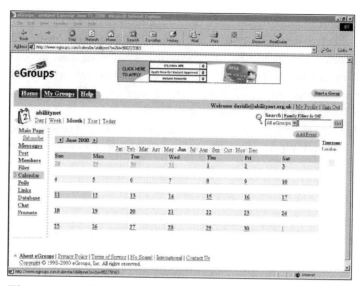

Figure 8.2   Calendar from www.eGroups.com

sending a memo to the whole school but as a member of staff opens their page they are told of today's events and those forthcoming.

Other individual and shared calendar services can be found by searching on the Web for free calendars or diaries (see Figures 8.1 and 8.2).

Documents

The distribution of documents to staff – especially those that are going through a number of drafts – can be a laborious task. The documents sections on the intranet allows anyone to post the latest draft of a document which all interested parties can download, read, comment on and e-mail back to the originator. Equally a weekly school newsletter or briefing can be posted for all to use. Figure 8.3 shows a page from AbilityNet.

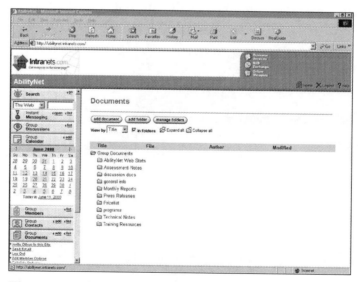

Figure 8.3   Intranets.com documents page

E-mail list

Sending individual e-mails to every contact you have can be almost as time-consuming as writing the letter by hand. An intranet allows you to send a message to all of the members or to sub-groups within the school (upper school, arts team, etc.). Staff prefer not to receive e-mails or memos that are not relevant to them and such a list can help hugely. A recent improvement to such a service is that every member of your staff team can now have an e-mail address based on your school name, e.g. David@yourschool.intranets.com.

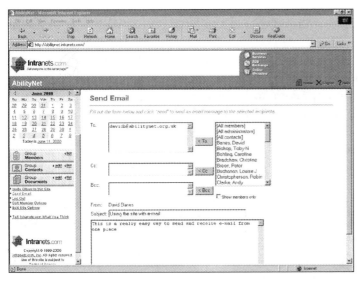

Figure 8.4   Intranets.com e-mail

A service such as onelist available from www.egroups.com offers further refinements in the form of a mailing list that members can either receive as individual mailings or as a daily digest. It has the added interest of having an established archive of every message that members can search at a later date (see Figure 8.5).

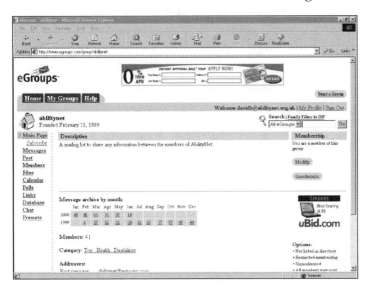

Figure 8.5   eGroups message archive

Group contacts

For any school there are a number of key contacts beyond the school that are of value to every member of staff. An electronic address book can be created within a site to allow e-mails to be sent directly to those key contacts – these could include the local educational psychologist, a voluntary organisation or ex-members of staff!

Links

The wealth of information that is available on the Web needs careful scanning. A lot of time can be saved for teams of staff if, when a good site is found, the member of staff shares this through a link on the intranet. As a good starting point we would recommend: www.meldrethmanor.com and www.abilitynet.co.uk

But then we would, wouldn't we!

News

At any time in a school events happen that it is important to communicate to everyone quickly. The news and announcements sections of an intranet site can be an extremely effective means of communicating with everyone, especially part-timers or staff who are away from school for any reason.

Other electronic communications

Forums

Beyond the structure of such a site as the one described above it is relatively easy to set up a school forum for discussion on themed issues. The strength of such a system is that all those interested in an issue – new maths curriculum – home school agreement, etc., can comment on an equal basis and their views can be added to by others through a thread (Figure 8.6).

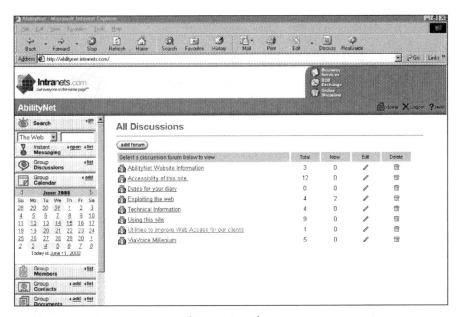

Figure 8.6   Intranets.com discussion forum

Other useful services

Xdrive – www.xdrive.com (monthly subscription)

For any school, class or teacher there is always a problem of sharing files between computers if you do not have a computer network established. If you have Internet connections to these computers one way around the problem is to use a service such as Xdrive which adds a drive of up to 100MB to your computer but is stored and accessed through the Internet. A small downloaded piece of software creates a drive icon in Windows Explorer which can be accessed like any other drive while you are connected to the Internet (see Figure 8.7).

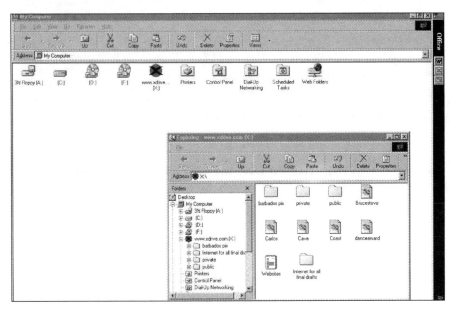

Figure 8.7   xdrives window

Internet for All

Current alternatives

www.all-the-free-space.com is a regularly updated list of free storage providers: we found www.kturn.com which, at the time of writing, offered 125MB of free space through the site.

Blink – www.blink.com (free service funded through advertising)

Blink is a similarly useful service, but operates by allowing any member of a team to upload their bookmarks (Netscape) or favourites (IE) to a central server where nominated others can access them. Hence if a member of a team finds a really useful site on Internet access they can upload it to Blink for others to use at their convenience. This is also very useful for teachers who have sites they want pupils to access but teach from a variety of classrooms, and as the site operates from your bookmarks, etc., you don't have to type in all the URLs.

Blink's public library of bookmarks is also a useful list of links on any specific issue that you might be interested in (Figure 8.8).

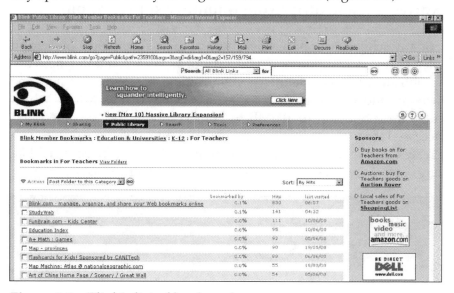

Figure 8.8 Blink's list of bookmarks

Genie – www.genie.co.uk (mostly free services)

As an example of how telecommunications and the Internet are converging, we can look at how a relatively new service might be used. Genie allows users to send a text message to any mobile phone for free, as long as the phone supports text messaging. For schools on large sites or split sites this can be a useful way for the school secretary to keep in touch with roving staff with a degree of ease. The message services offer a useful alternative to voice calls as they can be handled more discreetly as one does a pager.

112

Genie offers a wide range of other communications tools in addition. This includes the option to dictate a voicemail or text message to send to a mobile user, an online address book, a servicer for directing your e-mails to your mobile phone, as well as an online calendar and chat rooms.

This convergence between hand held and desktop devices is one which we can expect to see happening in much greater degrees over the coming years.

PalTalk (www.paltalk.com) (basic level free – advanced level small annual subscription)

Paltalk is an instant message service which allows person to person audio and video communications to take place. This can also be done with small groups of people and is available as a free download from the website. If you wish to have three webcams open at the same time you will need to pay the small annual subscription.

The service also offers access to paltalk servers in which rooms can be created for chats, files exchanged and audio/visual contacts established. These rooms can be open or by invited membership only.

Other useful software for similar communications include ICQ and Cu-seeme.

Figure 8.9

.Net (free)

The .net concept is a simple one. MSN and its affilates offer a range of services free or paid that can be accessed through the same username/password combination. These include Microsoft Reader; Microsoft.com; MS eLearningl; MSN Auctions; MSN Calendar; MSN Communities; MSN Hotmail; MSN Messenger; MSN Mobile; MSN MoneyCentral; MSN.com; as well as other services such as ebay, lastminute.com and even xdrive.

Having signed up for a hotmail account, users are automatically given a >net passport. This can be used to access the MSN homepage configured to your individual preferences. From this page instant messaging, e-mail, chat rooms are all available at the click of a mouse button. In addition other communication tools such as online photo albums, and MSN calendar are also available.

One of the most interesting of these is the option for MSN communities. Like intranets.com, these personalised areas offer closed membership web spaces in which staff can communicate and work with each other online.

Within each online community a manager can establish areas for chat, documents, photos, a message board, a shared calendar, and shared links. Users can have the option to have new additions to the community e-mailed to them individually as a daily digest or by accessing the website. This remains probably the very best of these free services.

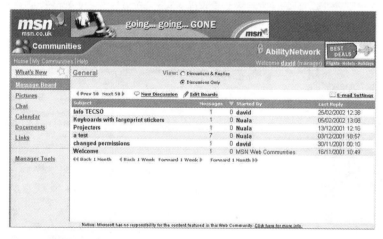

Figure 8.10   MSN Communities – message board

Figure 8.11 MSN – calendar

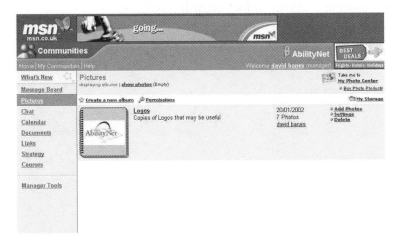

Figure 8.12 MSN – pictures

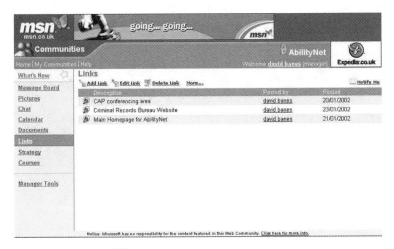

Figure 8.13 MSN – links

Summary

Schools evolve through debate and discussion, but under growing pressure of time it is increasingly difficult to involve everyone in a staff team in discussion in a meaningful way. Sites such as these are useful tools to allow your team to be involved, without producing mountains of paper and by encouraging people to contribute to those discussions and decisions that they are most interested in rather than anything and everything.

Connectivity is crucial as schools change and we develop outreach services. In recent years one of the authors has worked extensively with an FE college in Glasgow. This college has 100 outreach centres from which staff and linked tutors might operate. The potential for connecting these sites and staff together through the ways outlined above are extremely attractive.

We have looked at a small number of services quite specifically within this section because they have offered a unique package of services that we can recommend through experience over a lengthy period. Innovative use of integrating these packages with others is far from impossible and can in fact be quite exciting.

Chapter 9

The future

> The Internet will become invisible – you will not be able to tell where it begins or where it ends.

To predict the future we need to appreciate the history. We have often discussed with teachers the pace of technological change, usually in the context of how the computers the school bought two years ago are now nearly obsolete, but we tend to only be able to judge the acceleration in the short term. If we look back at the rate of innovation in developing the Internet over the past 40 years, the acceleration becomes even more apparent.

Let us look at a timeline of events (the following is reproduced with the permission of its author, David Kristula, and can be found at www.davesite.com).

1957

The USSR launches Sputnik, the first artificial earth satellite. In response, the United States forms the Advanced Research Projects Agency (ARPA) within the Department of Defense (DoD) to establish US lead in science and technology applicable to the military.
Backbones: None – Hosts: None

1962

Paul Baran, of the RAND Corporation (a government agency), was commissioned by the US Air Force to do a study on how it could maintain its command and control over its missiles and bombers, after a nuclear attack. This was to be a military research network that could survive a nuclear strike, decentralised so that if any locations (cities) in the US were attacked, the military could still have control of nuclear arms for a counter-attack.

Baran's finished document described several ways to accomplish this. His final proposal was a packet switched network.

'*Packet switching is the breaking down of data into datagrams or packets that are labeled to indicate the origin and the destination of the information and the forwarding of these packets from one computer to another computer until the information arrives at its final destination computer. This was crucial to the realization of a computer network. If packets are lost at any given point, the message can be resent by the originator.*'
Backbones: None – Hosts: None

1968

ARPA awarded the ARPANET contract to BBN. BBN had selected a Honeywell minicomputer as the base on which they would build the switch. The physical network was constructed in 1969, linking four nodes: University of California at Los Angeles, SRI (in Stanford), University of California at Santa Barbara, and University of Utah. The network was wired together via 50 Kbps circuits.
Backbones: 50Kbps ARPANET – Hosts: 4

1972

The first e-mail program was created by Ray Tomlinson of BBN.

The Advanced Research Projects Agency (ARPA) was renamed The Defense Advanced Research Projects Agency (or DARPA).

ARPANET was currently using the Network Control Protocol or NCP to transfer data. This allowed communications between hosts running on the same network.
Backbones: 50Kbps ARPANET – Hosts: 23

1973

Development began on the protocol later to be called TCP/IP, it was developed by a group headed by Vinton Cerf from Stanford and Bob Kahn from DARPA. This new protocol was to allow diverse computer networks to interconnect and communicate with each other.
Backbones: 50Kbps ARPANET – Hosts: 23+

1984

The ARPANET was divided into two networks: MILNET and ARPANET. MILNET was to serve the needs of the military and ARPANET to support the advanced research component, Department of Defense continued to support both networks.

Upgrade to CSNET was contracted to MCI. New circuits would be T1 lines, 1.5 Mbps which is 25 times faster than the old 56 Kbps lines. IBM would provide advanced routers and Merit would manage the network. New network was to be called NSFNET

(National Science Foundation Network), and old lines were to remain called CSNET.
Backbones: 50Kbps ARPANET, 56Kbps CSNET, plus satellite and radio connections – Hosts: 1024

1985

The National Science Foundation began deploying its new T1 lines, which would be finished by 1988.
Backbones: 50Kbps ARPANET, 56Kbps CSNET, 1.544Mbps (T1) NSFNET, plus satellite and radio connections – Hosts: 1961

1986

The Internet Engineering Task Force or IETF was created to serve as a forum for technical coordination by contractors for DARPA working on ARPANET, US Defense Data Network (DDN), and the Internet core gateway system.
Backbones: 50Kbps ARPANET, 56Kbps CSNET, 1.544Mbps (T1) NSFNET, plus satellite and radio connections – Hosts: 2308

1987

BITNET and CSNET merged to form the Corporation for Research and Educational Networking (CREN), another work of the National Science Foundation.
Backbones: 50Kbps ARPANET, 56Kbps CSNET, 1.544Mbps (T1) NSFNET, plus satellite and radio connections – Hosts: 28,174

1988

Soon after the completion of the T1 NSFNET backbone, traffic increased so quickly that plans immediately began on upgrading the network again.
Backbones: 50Kbps ARPANET, 56Kbps CSNET, 1.544Mbps (T1) NSFNET, plus satellite and radio connections – Hosts: 56,000

1990

(Updated 8/2001) Merit, IBM and MCI formed a not for profit corporation called ANS, Advanced Network & Services, which was to conduct research into high speed networking. It soon came up with the concept of the T3, a 45 Mbps line. NSF quickly adopted the new network and by the end of 1991 all of its sites were connected by this new backbone.

While the T3 lines were being constructed, the Department of Defense disbanded the ARPANET and it was replaced by the NSFNET backbone. The original 50Kbs lines of ARPANET were taken out of service.

Tim Berners-Lee and CERN in Geneva implements a hypertext system to provide efficient information access to the members of the international high-energy physics community.

Backbones: 56Kbps CSNET, 1.544Mbps (T1) NSFNET, plus satellite and radio connections – Hosts: 313,000

1991

CSNET (which consisted of 56Kbps lines) was discontinued having fulfilled its important early role in the provision of academic networking service. A key feature of CREN is that its operational costs are fully met through dues paid by its member organisations.

The NSF established a new network, named NREN, the National Research and Education Network. The purpose of this network is to conduct high speed networking research. It was not to be used as a commercial network, nor was it to be used to send a lot of the data that the Internet now transfers.
Backbones: Partial 45Mbps (T3) NSFNET, a few private backbones, plus satellite and radio connections – Hosts: 617,000

1992

Internet Society is chartered.

World Wide Web released by CERN.

NSFNET backbone upgraded to T3 (44.736Mbps)
Backbones: 45Mbps (T3) NSFNET, private interconnected backbones consisting mainly of 56Kbps, 1.544Mbps, plus satellite and radio connections – Hosts: 1,136,000

1993

InterNIC created by NSF to provide specific Internet services: directory and database services (by AT&T), registration services (by Network Solutions Inc.), and information services (by General Atomics/CERFnet).

Marc Andreessen and NCSA and the University of Illinois develops a graphical user interface to the WWW, called 'Mosaic for X'.
Backbones: 45Mbps (T3) NSFNET, private interconnected backbones consisting mainly of 56Kbps, 1.544Mbps, and 45Mpbs lines, plus satellite and radio connections – Hosts: 2,056,000

1994

No major changes were made to the physical network. The most significant thing that happened was the growth. Many new networks were added to the NSF backbone. Hundreds of thousands of new hosts were added to the INTERNET during this time period.

Pizza Hut offers pizza ordering on its Web page.

First Virtual, the first cyberbank, opens.

ATM (Asynchronous Transmission Mode, 145Mbps) backbone is installed on NSFNET.
Backbones: 145Mbps (ATM) NSFNET, private interconnected backbones consisting mainly of 56Kbps, 1.544Mbps, and 45Mpbs lines, plus satellite and radio connections – Hosts: 3,864,000

1995

The National Science Foundation announced that as of 30 April 1995 it would no longer allow direct access to the NSF backbone. The National Science Foundation contracted with four companies that would be providers of access to the NSF backbone (Merit). These companies would then sell connections to groups, organisations, and companies.

$50 annual fee is imposed on domains, excluding .edu and .gov domains which are still funded by the National Science Foundation.

Backbones: 145Mbps (ATM) NSFNET (now private), private interconnected backbones consisting mainly of 56Kbps, 1.544Mbps, 45Mpbs, 155Mpbs lines in construction, plus satellite and radio connections – Hosts: 6,642,000

1996 to present

Most Internet traffic is carried by backbones of independent ISPs, including MCI, AT&T, Sprint, UUnet, BBN planet, ANS, and more.

Currently the Internet Society, the group that controls the Internet, is trying to figure out new TCP/IP to be able to have billions of addresses, rather than the limited system of today. The problem that has arisen is that it is not known how both the old and the new addressing systems will be able to work at the same time during a transition period.
Backbones: 145Mbps (ATM) NSFNET (now private), private interconnected backbones consisting mainly of 56Kbps, 1.544Mbps, 45Mpbs, and 155Mpbs lines, plus satellite and radio connections – Hosts: over 15,000,000, and growing rapidly

Users in almost 150 countries around the world are now connected to the Internet. Since 2000 the rate of acceleration has increased still further. E-commerce has grown and is anticipated to become a multi-billion pound industry in three years, commercial sites now outweigh educational sites many times over, and yet the Internet is still in its infancy.

No one can tell you where the Internet will be in five years time. We know it is dynamic, we know it is increasingly pervading all aspects of our daily lives. A review of the discussions currently taking place within the Internet community demonstrates this all-pervasive nature. One search took me to discussions on the impact on politics and elections, to the impact upon the media, on shopping and personal relationships – the list was endless.

Three factors lead us inexorably towards this conclusion: the first is the trend to 'convergence'; that is, the pressure for all forms of communication to converge into one interface. Your PC can play music on a CD or MP3 format, your television can browse the Web, you can watch TV on your PC, you can e-mail from your mobile phone, you can SMS message a telephone from the Web, etc. The pressure to find small, simple, single interfaces is growing and we can expect this to accelerate still further in the future.

The second factor is embedded technology. As interfaces simplify so there will be increasing development of the 'connected home' (and by inference the connected school), in which we can interact through the Internet with the buildings in which we work, play and live. A scenario in which we e-mail our oven to tell it we are an hour from home so please cook the dinner is within grasp, and with the advent of GPS (Global Positioning Satellite) we can take this a stage further and have the cooker informed that we are held up in traffic, so reduce the oven temperature until we are moving again.

Another example of embedded technology can be seen in the development of voice recognition technology. What was once seen as a toy for the desktop, or in the imagination of science fiction buffs, is now used daily by people with and without disabilities to access their PC, to write letters and even surf the Web. This technology is now embedded into mobile phones. When I tell my phone to answer, it recognises the command and allows me to make a connection to an incoming call. Again, to use our cooking example, it cannot be long until one can activate everyday devices in the home in the same way, 'Oven start 16.00 hours cook 90 minutes temperature 200 degrees,' and so on.

The third factor is globalisation. While the rate of acceleration is not consistent across either the developed nations or under-developed countries, there is without doubt an inexorable growth towards connectivity. On the Web I explored the statistics for connections in Bangladesh, I spoke to a museum in Namibia which is connecting the nation's schools, and I watched live transmissions of webcam images from every continent. As satellite connections become achievable, and these are already available to purchase, so I will be able to pick up my e-mail anywhere in the world in which I can see the sky.

Implications for society

The implications for us as a society, in the ways in which we manage ourselves, the ways in which we interact with people, and the way in which we access and use information, are immense. However, the issue we want to consider is the implications for schools and the implications for people with a disability.

We want to accentuate the positive. If we look at the nature of people who use the Internet, there are many aspects that are satisfying. Hauben and Hauben (1998) (http://www.firstmonday.dk/issues/issue37/ chapter1/, The Net and Netizens: The impact of the net on people's lives), used the term 'Netizens' to describe the users of online communities. These communities were characterised by welcoming intellectual activity, by interpersonal relationships that were friendly and supportive, even where this help involved illegal activity such as sending programs to those who needed them. The net in this vision represented an untapped resource which offered a unique opportunity.

> Every user of the Net gains the role of being special and useful. The fact that every user has his or her own opinions and interests adds to the general body of specialized knowledge on the Net. Each Netizen thus becomes a special resource valuable to the Net. Each user contributes to the whole intellectual and social value and possibilities of the Net. (Hauben and Hauben 1998)

This principle is dependent upon the notion of universal access. Barriers to universal access – cultural, political, economic, physical or technological – prevent the Net achieving this goal. The disadvantaged in society, including those with disabilities, while disenfranchised limit the potential of the Net, and in turn they are limited by constraints beyond their control.

The information on the Web is not in the hands of large corporations or governments; despite the growth of e-commerce vast portions of the information on the Web are in the hands of the users of the Web. This includes children and includes those with disabilities. This information may be one-sided or even wrong. Traditional media demand that errors are removed, all information should be accurate and objective; but sociologists would argue that all information is culturally influenced, and Hauben and Hauben's Netizens offers an alternative solution:

> When you get more information from diverse sources, you don't always . . . get more accurate information. However, you do develop skills in discerning accurate information . . . Or rather, you do if you want to come out of the info-glut jungle alive . . .

The Web then, offers societies the opportunity to broaden their experience. We have been fortunate to meet friends from across the world as a result of our discussions about the Internet and about disability on the Internet. The children and young adults we supported were able to meet others around the world through e-mail and newsgroups that would otherwise have been unavailable to them.

Jean-Yves Djamen (1995) in http://www.sas.upenn.edu/ African_Studies/Padis/telmatics_Djamen.html, *Networking in Africa: An unavoidable evolution towards the Internet*, comments that: 'The impact of the Internet on daily life may be summarized into three major components: communication between individuals, promotion of new activities, and lifting of transnational borders.'

This is not to deny the problems that still emerge. The anonymity of the Web while offering a positive freedom also allows some to abuse those they meet. The heavy imbalance of men to women as Net users has led some women to feel threatened while online. The challenge of new means of allowing social exclusion are all issues which will need to be considered over the coming years.

Implications for schools

These issues have obvious implications for schools throughout the world. Schools will need to teach children to protect themselves and their property online, but also to be able to discern the nuances of fact and the bias that any feature may present. This is a high order skill: many adults accept the version of reality presented by the media as 'gospel' ranging from 'Freddie Starr Ate my Hamster' to a saintly vision of Diana, Princess of Wales, without question and will vigorously reject alternative realties that contradict.

The commonly held view therefore of schools adopting a whitelist approach to information on the Web creates a dilemma in failing to prepare children and young adults for the contradictions they face in the future.

We will need to face the opportunity for greater distance interpersonal communications. For some, many of their relationships may be initiated or extended across the Web. Universities have already acknowledged the power of distance learning to enable access to Higher Education to many, and there will come a point where the relationship between learning at home and learning at school will become blurred by the ability to utilise technology to connect the two. This blurring will affect both the range of learning that takes place, with a greater emphasis in schools upon the institution as the locus for activities that require a physical presence and which promote physical/social interactions between people. This will also affect the hours in which schools and institutions operate.

That there has been, and will continue to be, a major impact of the Internet upon schools is validated repeatedly. Recognising that it is commonly held that Europe is at least two years behind the US in the development of the infrastructure to support the Web, we can look at the 1998 Nebraska evaluation of the Internet upon Schools, by Drs Neal W. Topp, Neal Grandgenett, Elliott Ostler and Robert Mortenson, University of Nebraska at Omaha (1998), http://ois.unomaha.edu/esu98/ESU98paper.htm, and appreciate the remarkable growth.

Connectivity in Nebraskan schools

Over 88% of the state's school buildings and classrooms have directly connected computers.

Nebraska teachers are increasing their use of the Internet each year. The data from responding web-using teachers in the May 1998 survey indicated that over 80% used e-mail daily and over 96% used e-mail at least weekly. Even when all the teachers in the seven counties were surveyed, the data showed 64% used e-mail at least weekly. Use of the

Web is also increasing, with over 89% indicating that they use the Web at least weekly.

Teachers are indicating that they are becoming more comfortable with integrating Internet, with over 69% of the surveyed teachers agreeing with a survey item, 'I feel comfortable with designing lessons that integrate Internet.' Teachers from around the state show that they are eager to learn more about effective strategies to infuse the Internet into their curriculum, as shown by the large number of staff development sessions held in the past few years, as well as the attendance count of 950 educators at the annual Midwest Internet Institute held in Lincoln in early August.

Looking at the attitudes of managers it was reported that:

1. Support by school principals for using the Internet with students is increasing. Since he/she is the instructional leader of a school, the principal's encouragement to use an instructional tool is important. Only 1% of the teacher respondents in 1998 indicated that their principal did *not* encourage them to use the Internet with students, a considerable reduction from the 19% of teacher respondents in 1997.
2. Schools are connected. In verification of school access to the Internet, 99.7% of the principals (290 out of 291) reported that their school was connected to the Internet.
3. The use of electronic mail was seen as an 'essential' component of principals' Internet use, with 88.7% of the principals reporting that the use of electronic mail is now 'very important' or 'somewhat important' to their current job activities.
4. The use of the World Wide Web was seen as growing in importance, with 97.6% of the principals reporting that the World Wide Web would be an important tool for them within the next five years.

Reviewing student use it was found that:

1. Student use is increasing. Almost 80% of the respondents reported that they had their students use the Internet. This is about a 20% increase over last year's responses. The reasons for not using the Internet with students were lack of available Internet-connected computers and incomplete or evolving school district policy on student use. It should be noted that few stated that 'the Internet was of little value in my classes'.
2. The Internet is being used in all subject areas and at all grade levels. Over 600 Internet-infused lesson plans were submitted by Nebraska teachers in the May 1998 survey and all subject areas and all grade levels were represented.
3. The impact of Internet on student learning seems positive. As with any new tool used in classrooms, the value of the innovation must be constantly evaluated. Although it is very difficult to measure the impact of the Internet on student progress, the 929 teachers of the 1998 survey indicated that they felt Internet use had a positive impact on classroom activities.

It is not suprising therefore that the educators in Nebraska found that there was a real impact upon the events that were happening in the classroom.

1. Student use appears to be a critical component to 'innovative' curricular use. The most impressive and effective curricular uses of the Internet observed in classrooms identified by other teachers as 'innovative' typically involved putting the students online for the majority of the classroom's Internet-based activities. This included having the students do the research, help plan the activity and even do routine typing tasks. The classroom enthusiasm of 'involved' and 'motivated' students was often one of the most observable aspects of the more 'innovative' classrooms, and was often identified by teachers as a major outcome related to Internet use by students.

2. Innovative uses often blend the Internet into other curricular activities. Many of the most innovative and effective uses of the Internet access the Net as one of several educational technology tools, in the support of more traditional curricular goals (learning about geometry in math, learning about the weather in science etc.). It appears that the many effective uses of the Internet involve the use of this network as a relatively 'transparent' resource in the teaching and learning process. It was also interesting that in this task-oriented environment, teachers appeared to have relatively little concern for the possibility of students accessing offensive material.

3. Internet is often used in multi-disciplined projects. Many Internet infused lesson units include the blending of two or more disciplines, using constructivist and 'real world' teaching/learning strategies. Many Nebraska teachers are using established state and national Internet-based collaborative projects.

4. Multicultural resources available on the Internet are important. Many teachers are particularly excited about the potential for the Internet to help support the multicultural goals of schools. Several teachers remarked that using the Internet made it much easier to find lessons that blend multicultural aspects with traditional discipline-related topics. For instance, one mathematics teacher was using paintings from several different countries, accessed over the Internet, to help teach the geometric concept of tessellations, as well as talk about the use of geometry in other cultures.

5. Student 'research' using the Internet appears to be at a considerably higher level than in more traditional classroom activities. This type of research appears to be much richer than more traditional school library-based research. Often, classes not only retrieved textual information, but accessed and incorporated information from visual images (such as NASA moon images, or artworks from National galleries), online software programs (such as physics ray tracing, or biology frog dissection programs), and even communicated with online experts (such as a genetics scientist). The concept of 'student research' seemed to be more dynamic, and teachers reported that even the word 'research' appeared to be used more commonly by students. In addition, the Internet research appeared to be more

interactive, with students sharing information as well as retrieving it (such as when talking to content experts, or students at other sites).

6. Innovative classroom uses often accessed 'non-traditional' classroom resources. Most of the innovative classroom activities related to the Internet accessed information which was not typically available in other mediums or school-based library resources. For example, current pictures of Jupiter were downloaded by an elementary science class, and daily White House schedules were accessed by a high school social studies class. In some classroom activities, these 'non-traditional' resources also included students in other countries, such as Russia, Finland and Australia. Thus, many of the innovative classroom uses involved using the Internet to secure information not available, or not readily available, from traditional sources, such as the school textbook or library resources. In addition, resources from the traditional sources seemed to be used effectively and wisely.

There seems no doubt that Nebraska is an interesting benchmark for us to consider, and is acknowledged as being further advanced than many other US states, but it does offer a real benchmark as to where we can expect UK mainstream schools to be in the next three years.

The key issues that emerge from such studies challenge closed teaching methods, as the key element of education on the Web is to sift through information selecting and interpreting that which one believes to be relevant before developing an idea. Traditionally the teacher has held the answers, in an online education the teacher holds the signposts and an answer.

In addition an online education involves connecting to others outside of the classroom, school, country or culture. Schools will have to decide whether to embrace the diversity this implies with all its implicit challenges or whether to reject the model and see the Web solely as a tool to add to other information sources.

Issues for disability

We have spent much of this book discussing the impact of the Internet upon people with a disability at both individual and community levels, so we will not repeat those discussions here. There can be no doubt that many people with a disability are grasping the opportunities offered by the Internet, and that with careful planning the Internet can enhance the lives and educational experience of children with a wide range of disabilities. The interfaces between person and computer or other gateway, and the Internet, will become less and less skill-dependent. Research has shown that neural implants by which devices can be controlled are possible and a number of people with cerebral palsy report positive results from neural stimulators. Ultimately there is a strong belief therefore that the Internet has become and will increasingly be a major influence to promote the inclusion of all with a disability.

Special education–the implications

Teachers have to learn rapidly. In an era of overload in the educational system, the advent of this technology may prove to be the final straw for many.

This technology is different to other media by the nature of the interaction it promotes – no other comes close. Our schools as organisations will need to evolve across physical boundaries and teachers will have to extend the boundaries of their practice accordingly if the exploitation of the Web is to be of benefit to all.

One implication of such a perspective is that the debate about inclusion may well move away from being a debate about the physical location of education and towards a debate regarding quality, individual needs and curriculum. Without doubt, if more people report on successful experience of inclusion or specialisation the debate may become more meaningful.

If resources are shared and commonly available between schools, and between schools and other providers, the debate about which school a child attends may become less acrimonious and based more positively on the child's choice for the best social interactions rather than a parent's choice over the 'best' school. Equally, the role of parents in educating children with special needs may be further developed. Distance therapy support via webcam and interactive whiteboard is manageable, and parents will be able to seek alternative options for their children with greater ease.

With these thoughts in mind, the special school and SENCO in schools will become a crucial part of this network, allowing information to be summarised and ideas to be incorporated into schools or rejected as necessary. Teachers will have to maintain their own professional portfolio at an advanced level, and within this may find that they need to facilitate education in other settings rather than always teach directly.

The curriculum and most especially that of PSHE, will need to consider the implications of this information overload upon children, helping to teach discrimination skills as part of protection rather than simply 'no go tell'.

In summary, special schools will have to more closely integrate the use of the Web into not only the content of the curriculum, but also into their methods and styles of teaching. They will need to consider:

> Communication – tools, etiquette, language and diversity of audiences are all expanded within the technology currently available.
> Handling information – to select, integrate and synthesise opinion and fact.
> Enhanced real time information – web cams, 24-hour news services, satellite data are constantly changing – what was available yesterday will not be there tomorrow.
> Testing concepts – ideas, solutions and opinions can be defined, tested and redefined constantly through all of the collectivity of the Web.

At the end of the day, schools will continue to exist for the foreseeable future, they will continue to be a key source of the transmission of skills, knowledge and values, but will have to recognise the fact that the range of influences is changing and diversifying.

And finally...?

We cannot begin to judge where we will be in ten years. The experience of the past five years has led us to believe that there is a real danger of a fast and slow track of Web use in schools. Politicians' rhetoric is preventing real investment at a local level, and media scare stories about the risks are inducing a Web paranoia that may prevent meaningful debate between schools and the parents of the children attending.

Four years ago we were told that investing in a high speed internet connection for a special school was likely to be seen by OFSTED as a waste of money and subject to the whim of the head teacher. We genuinely hope that in 2002 no manager or LEA advisor will be guilty of such inability to understand both the actuality and potential of the Web.

It is our hope that this book has at least illustrated the power that the Internet offers and will give schools options to exploit that. Whatever else, the next few years promise to be an era of innovation and change in connected schools – so whatever else – some things never change.

Postscript to the Second edition

The challenge of writing a second edition to this book was not to find new material – but to choose what to retain. In between the development of the two books the Internet has fulfilled many of our expectations. For David, working for AbilityNet it has more or less replaced paper as the primary means of communication across an organisation. When I asked my team when did they last receive a paper memo most could not ever remember one. We doubt if the same can be said of schools, or for that matter of classrooms.

Following the events of September 11, we have seen a war fought, where for the first time it was possible to get more or less unrestricted access to opinions from across the world, from the liberal to the most extreme right wing opinions – and for the first time access to the views of one's enemy. The threat that emerged was not of opinions changing but of confusion as to who was the enemy and who was not. At the end of this chapter in our first edition we commented that schools would have to teach children to select relevant information. The diversity of opinion and 'fact' after the World Trade Centre illustrates precisely the need for schools to address this issue rapidly. Even if the school limits access to this information, internet cafes, home computers and libraries may not.

Appendix: Examples of accessible and symbol supported websites on the Internet

There are an increasing number of accessible websites designed for pupils who are using symbols to complement text.

There are links to some of them on the Widget symbol site:

http://www.widgit.com/switchweb/html/

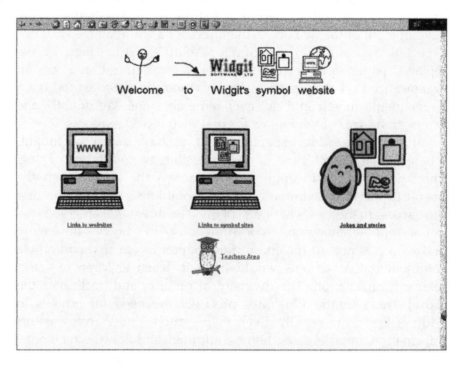

Following the links to symbol sites:

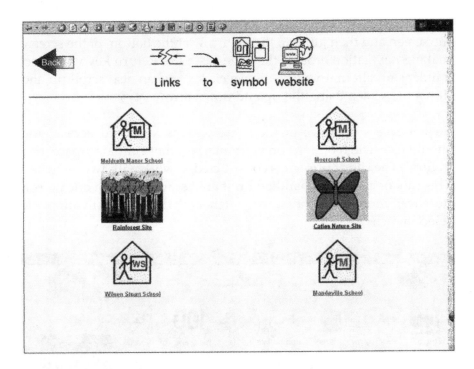

The Rainforest site has been designed to incorporate an additional access device in addition to having fully supported text.

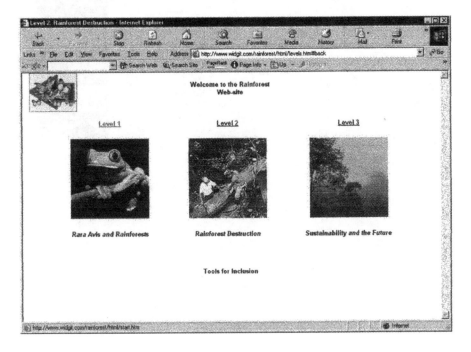

As the mouse pointer moves over a link, the link is highlighted by flowers or butterflies appearing. In Internet Explorer the scroll bar is also highlighted to make it easier for the user to scroll down the page.

The pages can be navigated using the Space bar and Return key. The Space bar will move the focus (shown by the flowers/butterflies appearing on any links). This will scan the two arrows at the top of the screen and then jump to the up arrow at the bottom of the screen, making navigation around the page easy. The Return key will select a link as an alternative to a mouse click. You can also scroll up and down the screen using the up and down arrow keys.

Switch access operates in the same way as keyboard access. You should use switch options on your interface that emulate 'Space' and 'return'. The site at present is constructed to work with two switches. This can, of course, be handled by shared scanning, with one person (teacher) controlling the scan switch and the user activating the select switch.

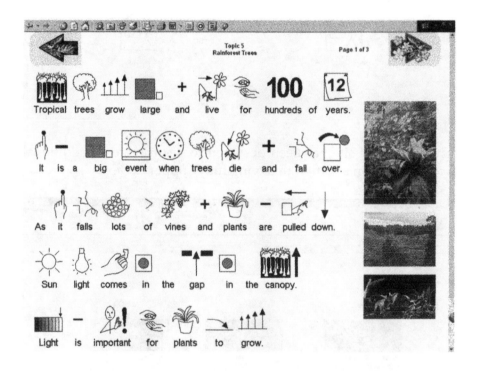

Glossary

Alt text   Alternative text allows a meaningful text alternative to graphics on a web page for readers who are using text-only web browsers. Speaking web browsers can also use the alternative text.

Cells (in overlay boards)   Areas on a touch sensitive overlay board that can be activated by touch.

Hotspots   An area of a document which, when the screen pointer is over it and clicked, tells the computer to go to another document or site.

HTML   Hypertext mark up language: the code used in documents to indicate how information is to be displayed on the World Wide Web. HTML files are read by a web browser which inteprets the codes about the format and size of text and pictures and where links to other files are to be placed.

Hypertext   Data that provides the links between pages on the Web, allowing you to move through pages and information non-sequentially.

e-mail   Electronic mail, sending and receiving messages over the Internet.

Internet browser   A program used on your computer to search and retrieve information on the Internet. Browsers allow you to click on links to another document, and move to a different computer where that resource is stored. The major browsers are Netscape Navigator and Internet Explorer.

IP   Internet protocol, part of the control mechanism of the Internet that defines the package structure of information sent over the Internet.

FTP   File transfer protocol, a tool for moving files from the Internet on to your computer, and for moving files from your computer on to the Internet.

Java   An object-orientated program language that can be integrated with web browsers to download and play Java programs.

Java script   A simple scripting language which is run by your browser and allows graphic effects and more interaction within the pages.

mouse over   A facility to activate a link automatically when the screen pointer is over it, without additional clicking.

overlay boards   A flat board that has a touch-sensitive surface. It can be used as an input device alongside the keyboard.

screen reader   Software that will interpret screen information as computer speech.

switches   A simple input device that is activated by pressing a surface which makes an electrical contact between two contacts.

TCP   Transmission control protocol, part of the control mechanisms that underpins the internet, enabling different computers to talk a common language.

TCP/IP   The complete tranmission control protocol/Internet protocol.

universal guidelines   A set of design principles that have clearly stated principles and definitions.

URL   Uniform resource locator. A standard way of refering to resources on the Internet. It specifies the exact location of the directory or file on the World Wide Web.

Web browser   The software program you need to find, retrieve and send information over the Internet.

W3C   The international body that tries to keep HTML standards so that HTML documents will work on different computer platforms and different browsers. Trying to ensure that the Web does not devolve into a proprietary world of incompatible formats.

References

Djamen, J.Y. (1995) www.sas.upenn.edu.African_studies/Padis/telmatics_Djamen.html
Hauben and Hauben (1998) *The Net and Netizens* www.first monday.dk/isuues/issue3_7/chapter1/PBS
pbs (1999) *Life on The Internet* www.pbs.org
Topp *et al.* (1998) ois.unomaha.edu/esu98/esu98paper.htm – Connectivity in Schools

Useful Websites

www.abilitynet.co.uk
www.arts4all.co.uk
www.becta.org.uk
www.bigscripts.com
www.blink.com
www.bravenet.com
www.cast.org
www.downloads.com
www.egroups.com
www.freeserve.co.uk
www.fultonpublishers.co.uk
www.hotmail.com
www.cita.gov.uk/iagc/rtfs/websites.rtf
www.ice-network.com
www.indpendentliving.org
www.intranets.com
www.java-scripts.net
www.listbot.com
www.loonyverse.com
www.meldrethmanor.com
www.nasen.org.uk
www.netguide.com/special/inernet/chat/howto/types
    html
www.peoplefirst.org.uk
www.quios.com
www.rnib.org.uk
www.safekids.com
www.thefreesite.com
www.the-times.co.uk
www.tripod.lycos.com
www.tucows.com
http://.uk.dir.yahoo.com/education/special_education/
www.xdrive.com
www.yahoo.com

Software and Hardware

Clicker4
Available from Crick Computing

Clickit
Available from Inclusive Technology

Switch access to windows
Available from Ace Centre

Windows switch
Available from Advisory Unit

Discovery switch
Available from Don Johnstone www.inclusive.co.uk

Surfmonkey
Available from www.surfmonkey.com

Internet Explorer
Available from www.microsoft.com

Opera
Available from
www.operasoftware.com

Bobby
Available from www.cast.org

Netscape
Available from www.netscape.com

Eudora
Available from www.eudora.com

Outlook
Available from www.microsoft.com

ws-ftp
Available from www.ipswitch.com

icq
Available from www.icq.com

Qtalk
Available from www.qtalk.com

HoneyQ
Available from www.honeysw.com

Netmeeting
Available from www.microsoft.com

RocketTalk
Available from www.rocketdownload.com

CU-Seeme
Available from www.cuseeme.com

Togglemouse
Available from www.toggle.com

Index